"Like a good detective novel, Michelle Skeen's book will help you uncover the mystery of your difficult relationship. After reading this book, you'll understand how your childhood experiences still affect your life, but more importantly, you'll learn what you can do to put them behind you and move on."

—Jeffrey C. Wood, PsyD, psychologist and coauthor of *The Dialectical Behavior Therapy Skills Workbook*

"The couples in successful relationships will tell you that, in order to succeed, partners must learn to work on their relationships. *The Critical Partner* is the ideal workbook to help couples who are dealing with this uncomfortable dynamic. It will teach them how to do what is necessary to make their relationship successful."

—Barton Goldsmith, PhD, author of *Emotional Fitness for Couples* and *Emotional Fitness for Intimacy*

"*The Critical Partner* is required reading for anyone living in a relationship where they feel frequently hurt, devalued, or blamed. This book will show you why this happens and give you tools to do something about it. Highly recommended."

—Matthew McKay, PhD, author of *Thoughts and Feelings*

"The most challenging issue in the life of the couple can be learning how to express disappointment and hurt without hurting your partner. Michelle Skeen offers an effective framework for understanding and dealing with the ruptures and self-defeating consequences of criticism in a relationship. She carefully applies the thoughtfully designed elements of schema therapy to her keen knowledge of this subject matter and offers her readers easily accessible strategies for transforming painful life patterns into healthy responses."

—Wendy T. Behary, LCSW, author of *Disarming The Narcissist*

D1234230

the
critical
partner

How to End the Cycle of Criticism & Get the *Love* You Want

Michelle Skeen, PsyD
Foreword by Jeffrey Young, PhD

New Harbinger Publications, Inc.

Publisher's Note

Distributed in Canada by Raincoast Books

Copyright © 2011 by Michelle Skeen
New Harbinger Publications, Inc.
5674 Shattuck Avenue
Oakland, CA 94609
www.newharbinger.com

Cover design by Amy Shoup; Acquired by Catharine Meyers; Edited by Nelda Street

Printed in the United States of America

Library of Congress Cataloging-in-Publication Data

Skeen, Michelle.
 The critical partner : how to end the cycle of criticism and get the love you want /
Michelle Skeen.
     p. cm.
 Includes bibliographical references and index.
 ISBN 978-1-60882-027-6 (pbk. : alk. paper) -- ISBN 978-1-60882-028-3 (pdf e-book :
alk. paper)
 1. Criticism, Personal. 2. Interpersonal conflict. 3. Couples--Psychology. 4. Man-
woman relationships--Psychology. I. Title.
 BF637.C74S54 2011
 158.2'4--dc23
                            2011029637

13   12   11

10   9   8   7   6   5   4   3   2   1

First printing

This book is dedicated to my children: Eric, Jake, and Kelly. Your love, support, humor, intelligence, and appreciation serve as a constant reminder of what is important and possible in life. I love you deeply.

Contents

Foreword

I t is a great pleasure to write this foreword to The Critical Partner. It is
gratifying to read an excellent expansion of the schema therapy approach
that can help so many people who are in painful, destructive relationships
because they have partners who are highly critical of them.

A common issue among couples is criticism. I frequently work with
couples in which one partner in the relationship is openly and consistently
critical of the other (the "critical" partner). Over time this interaction has
a destructive effect on the relationship, and on the well-being of the partner who is the victim of the criticism (the "vulnerable" partner). Often
both partners in a relationship become locked into a maladaptive, repeti-
tive cycle that they don't understand and find difficult to change.

This book first provides the reader with a way of understanding these
destructive cycles through the concepts of schema therapy and the use of
our assessment tools. Readers learn new and more effective strategies,
based on schema therapy principles, to change the critical partner and to
break their self-defeating patterns of interaction.

Using schema therapy as a framework, you will gain a deeper understanding of yourself, your partner, and the early childhood experiences in
both of your families that shaped the relationship you are in. This deeper
understanding of your own early maladaptive schemas, as well as those of

your critical partner, will enable each of you to view the other with a level of compassion that you did not have before.

Michelle first presents case studies of couples that are in crisis as a primary result of the critical behavior of one partner. Each of the stories illustrates one of the five primary schemas of the critical partner. This is followed with assessment tools you can use to determine your partner's schemas. This assessment process is informative and empathy-building. It highlights what I consider one of the real strengths of the schema approach: developing compassion for ourselves and others through understanding our early maladaptive schemas, and how they developed as a result of painful childhood and adolescent experiences.

The next section of the book presents case studies of the five primary schemas in the vulnerable partner, along with assessment tools to help you figure out your own primary schemas. Michelle then explains the importance of coping behaviors. Coping behaviors are responses to schema triggering events that we all develop as ways to protect ourselves when we feel we are under threat. However, in the long run, these coping behaviors cause harm to ourselves and to our partners.

The final two chapters deal with change. Michelle teaches new coping strategies you can use to deal with your schemas and with your partner in healthier ways. You will also learn how to react to schema triggering situations more effectively.

Changing our intimate relationships is not easy. Our emotions, beliefs, and behaviors began early in our lives and are now deeply entrenched. Nevertheless I am confident that readers of this book who have critical partners can make dramatic progress in improving their relationships by working hard to understand and then follow the principles outlined in this book. Doing this requires patience and compassion, but the payoff in improving your relationship will make all the effort you put in worthwhile.

—Jeffrey Young, Ph.D.

Acknowledgments

It would not have been possible for me to write this book without my mentor, colleague, and friend Matt McKay. Matt introduced me to Jeffrey Young's schema-focused theory. Matt's intelligence, insight, humor, and energy are inspiring. Thank you, Matt.

I would also like to thank Jeffrey Young for the brilliant theory on which he founded schema-focused therapy, a theory I have had the privilege of seeing him present on numerous occasions. His presentation is nothing short of compelling. Jeff, it is a dream come true that you agreed to write the foreword for my book. Thank you.

My heartfelt thanks go to my friends, who each share with me their own brand of intelligence, humor, and insight. I love you. To my mother, thank you for your love and support. To John, thank you for everything that you have taught me through words and actions over the years. Your combination of integrity, intelligence, passion, and humor is incomparable. And, a special thanks to four of my friends who bore the burden of managing my anxiety during the creation of this book—Jarek, Art, Sarah, and Jeff. Thank you for not changing your phone numbers.

To all of my clients over the past eight years, thank you for opening your hearts to me and sharing your very personal and special stories. I value everything that you have brought to me. I am a better person and a better therapist for the experience.

To all of the staff at New Harbinger Publications, thank you for your guidance during this process. A special thanks goes to Catharine Meyers for thinking of me when she conceived of this book, as well as for her support and encouragement. And to Nelda Street, thank you for your guidance and expertise during the copyediting process.

Introduction

If you are in a relationship with someone who you feel is a critical partner, if you feel as if your partner unfairly judges you, if you feel that your partner routinely criticizes you for things that are blown out of proportion or beyond your control, or if you feel that your partner consistently looks for things about you to criticize, then this book is for you.

A common and destructive part of many relationships, criticism is particularly hurtful when it attacks your personality or character, threatening your self-esteem. This book will help you if you feel criticized or perhaps even verbally abused by your partner. It is not meant to help people whose partners threaten violence or are physically abusive. Please seek immediate professional help if your safety is compromised.

This book provides the skills and self-knowledge that you will need to make some necessary changes in your relationship. Making these positive changes in your relationship will take time, perseverance, consistency, and strength. You will need to commit to helping you and your partner get to a healthier and happier place in your relationship. When you adopt the alternative coping strategies that are explained in this book, your partner's interactions with you will change whether or not she is consciously aware of your changed behavior. If your partner has expressed a desire to change the critical and angry behavior, then you may choose to include him in the assessment and exercises presented in this book. If your partner won't acknowledge having a critical attitude or becomes defensive when you discuss your experience, then it may be best for you to use the book on your own and make the changes unilaterally. Either way, when you make the suggested changes in your interactions with your partner, you'll notice her changing in response.

Chapter 1

Understanding Your Critical Partner

The first step toward disarming your critical partner is to gain a greater understanding of how he thinks. This is an essential part of making the necessary changes that will lead to an improved relationship. One way to achieve this goal is to look at your partner's *schemas*, which are core beliefs that are rooted in early childhood and stay with us throughout our lives. Core beliefs define who we are, our interactions with others, our partner selection, our emotional reactions to situations, and our worldviews. Every experience we have potentially interacts with our core beliefs and those of others. Our schemas, or core beliefs, direct how we live our lives and also create the internal monologue that contains personal thoughts, assumptions, and interpretations that inform our individual worldviews. Core beliefs guide us in establishing the rules by which we live. A schema is a very stable and enduring pattern that consists of memories, body sensations, emotions, and cognitions. When a schema is activated, it will produce intense emotions. Understanding the rules that drive your partner's behavior can lead you to adopt healthier coping and communication strategies between you and your partner.

Early Core Childhood Needs

Unmet early childhood needs create negative schemas. According to Jeffrey Young (2004), there are six needs that must be met for a child to thrive. If these needs are neglected, they create schemas that become problematic for you and your critical partner. As explained below, five of the schemas specific to you and your critical partner will form as a result of unmet childhood needs. Note that some of the schemas are not mentioned again in the book. The schemas that are highlighted are the most relevant schemas for you and your critical partner.

- *Basic safety:* Essential at birth, this need involves how the child is treated by her own family. When an infant or child is not provided with a stable and safe environment, either one or both of the following early maladaptive schemas will form: abandonment, and mistrust and abuse.

- *Connection to others:* When a child doesn't receive love, affection, empathy, understanding, and guidance from family members or peers, emotional deprivation or social exclusion schemas, or both, can develop.

- *Autonomy:* This is essential for childhood development and allows for healthy independence and separation from parents. When a child is not taught self-reliance, responsibility, and good judgment, he will likely develop dependence or vulnerability schemas.

- *Self-esteem:* When children are loved, accepted, and respected, they develop self-esteem. But in the absence of family and peer support during childhood, the early maladaptive schemas of defectiveness, failure, or both will develop.

- *Self-expression:* In a nurturing environment, children are encouraged to express their needs and desires. When this self-expression is discouraged, children are made to feel that their needs and feelings matter less than those of their parents. Often the child is punished and made to feel "less than." When a child's self-expression isn't encouraged and supported, she can develop the early maladaptive schemas of subjugation and unrelenting standards.

- *Realistic limits:* When parents are permissive and overindulgent, the child will grow up without experiencing realistic limits and without understanding the need to consider other people before acting. In the absence of realistic limits, the early maladaptive schema of entitlement develops.

Your critical partner's maladaptive schemas are the result of one or more of these unmet childhood needs.

Common Schemas of the Critical Partner

This book presents five critical partner schemas. The following descriptions are designed to assist you in identifying which profile best describes your critical partner. You may find the stories presented with each schema to be useful in recognizing familiar behaviors and interactions. The more structured assessments for identifying your critical partner's schema are presented in chapter 2.

Critical Partner Schema: Defectiveness and Shame

The core emotions of the critical partner with a defectiveness and shame schema are shame and fear. Someone with a defectiveness and shame schema has the worldview of being bad, unwanted, inferior, or invalid in important respects, or fears possibly becoming unlovable to a partner if his true self were exposed (Young 2004). The coping behavior of people who are overcompensating for this schema is to be critical of others, act superior, or try to present as being perfect. Paradoxically, the more these people are loved, the more critical they can become of their partners.

♥ Beth and Joe's Story

Beth was initially attracted to Joe because he was kind, good looking, intelligent, and fun. They met in college, and Beth found him to be a refreshing alternative to the fraternity boys that she typically had dated. For Joe, Beth was the perfect package. She was beautiful, smart, and the only daughter of loving parents. At first, Joe was adoring and complimentary of Beth. She was everything that he had dreamed of in a partner. On the surface they appeared to be a good match. But Joe harbored deep shame about his family of origin. His parents had divorced when he was in first grade. Prior to the divorce, Joe's father had begun wearing women's clothing around the house. After moving out, Joe's dad had a sex-change operation and lived as a woman full-time.

Meanwhile, Joe was forced to be self-sufficient at a young age. Frequently he was left at day care until 8:00 p.m. and occasionally was "forgotten." As a teenager, Joe was kicked out of the home that he shared with his mother and younger sister (the favorite child). All of these childhood experiences made Joe feel inferior, unwanted, and unlovable. The closer that Beth and Joe became, the more vulnerable he was to his defectiveness and shame schema.

Both Beth and Joe find that he becomes critical of her after they spend time with her family and friends. Beth reports that in social situations, Joe criticizes everyone. He responds that he is joking, but his jokes have a hard edge that leaves everyone feeling uncomfortable. The discomfort others experience around Joe have Beth's family and friends questioning why Beth is with him. Although Beth loves Joe and knows that he is a good person, she feels that his behavior needs to change or she might eventually have to let go.

Critical Partner Schema: Entitlement

The core emotion of the critical partner with an entitlement schema is anger. The worldview of people with an entitlement schema is that they are superior to others and deserve special treatment. They want what they want and they want it now. When their desires are frustrated, they respond with irritation or worse. The coping behavior of these people is to be controlling, manipulative, and selfish toward others in their efforts to meet their own needs. They lack empathy, have rigid standards, are very competitive, feel superior, and seek approval (Young 2004).

♥ Camille and Tom's Story

Camille and Tom seem like the golden couple. They met while attending an Ivy League law school. Tom knew that he was attractive, intelligent, and pedigreed, and he would settle for nothing less in a partner. Camille adored Tom and seemed fine with his top-dog status in their relationship. Tom loved to be the center of attention. He was the only child of adoring and successful parents who always made him feel as if the world revolved around him. In fact, anyone who spent time in Tom's world began to believe it. Camille and Tom's relationship progressed: they completed law school, became engaged after graduation, and, a year later, had their wedding at the Plaza Hotel in New York City, where no expense was spared. Tom's parents insisted on paying for the wedding, as they wanted to ensure that it would be unforgettable. No detail was overlooked in the planning and the execution—only the best for Tom! No one was surprised when the golden couple announced that they were expecting a baby nine months after their romantic honeymoon. Camille and Tom appeared to have it all.

However, as Camille's pregnancy progressed, the spotlight often shifted from Tom to Camille and her growing "baby bump." Tom often became irritable and critical toward Camille when he returned home from a night out with friends. Camille wasn't bothered by Tom's little tantrums; she understood that he was accustomed to being the center of attention, and she did her best to make sure that he continued to get the attention that he demanded.

Everything changed when Camille began experiencing preterm contractions seven months into her pregnancy. Camille was quickly confined to bed rest for the remainder of her pregnancy. Tom's reaction to the news was not concern but irritation. Tom called Camille's doctor and demanded that he come up with an alternative solution that wouldn't require bed rest for Camille. When the doctor explained that there was no alternative, Tom's irritation turned to anger. Having to take bed rest meant Camille could no longer accommodate Tom's needs. Tom became more critical of Camille, and she was regularly subjected to his angry outbursts. At root, Tom lacked empathy for Camille, and when his desires went unmet, he lit into her.

Critical Partner Schema: Mistrust and Abuse

The core emotions of the critical partner with a mistrust and abuse schema are fear and anxiety. The worldview of people with a mistrust and abuse schema is that others cannot be trusted. Their coping behavior is to be guarded and suspicious. They tend to avoid sharing their innermost thoughts and feelings with others because they believe that others will use the information against them. They constantly test others to determine whether they can be trusted, and have a difficult time forming close relationships. When their schema is triggered, they can become abusive as a way to reassert control and protect themselves from being hurt (Young 2004).

♥ Ron and Elizabeth's Story

Ron met Elizabeth at the gym, where they both took kickboxing classes. Ron was drawn to Elizabeth's athleticism, competitive spirit, and bold sense of humor. In many ways, she came across as one of the guys: tough and fun. Nothing seemed off-limits. Their first interaction outside of the gym was in a group setting at a bar after their Wednesday night advanced kickboxing class. Ron had a great time with Elizabeth. They talked easily with one another, but on later reflection, he realized that he had revealed more about himself than she had offered about herself.

At the end of the night, he asked her out on a date, and she said yes. They dated for several months before becoming intimate with each other. Elizabeth made it clear that she wanted to take things slowly. Ron thought the first night that they stayed together in his apartment was perfect. The connection between the two of them felt wonderful. When they were lying in bed holding each other, Elizabeth began to quietly sob. Ron held her closer, touched by the emotion that she was expressing.

The next morning he brought her coffee in bed. Everything seemed fine until his phone rang. Ron didn't want to interrupt their time together, so he chose not to answer. Unexpectedly, Elizabeth flew into a rage and accused Ron of not answering his phone because he was hiding a relationship with another woman. Ron was stunned by her volatile mood swings: crying the previous night and exploding that morning. What Ron didn't understand at the time was that Elizabeth had grown up in a household where her mother was emotionally abusive and her father was physically abusive. The intimacy that Ron and Elizabeth shared made Elizabeth vulnerable to her core worldview that others could not be trusted and that if she let her guard down, she would get hurt.

Critical Partner Schema: Abandonment

The core emotions of the critical partner with an abandonment schema are anxiety, sadness, depression, and anger toward people who leave them. Their worldview is that important people will leave them, behave unpredictably, or get sick and die (Young 2004). The coping behaviors of people who are overcompensating for an abandonment schema include clinging to partners, being jealous and possessive, attacking, withdrawing, and controlling.

♥ Brad and Lisa's Story

Brad and Lisa, both in their early thirties, were working for an international investment bank in New York when they met and fell in love. They moved in together after six months of dating and married a year later. Brad and Lisa spent an enormous amount of time together. Their offices were on the same floor, and outside of work they exercised together, socialized with friends together, and had quiet evenings at home together.

Two years into their marriage, Brad was offered a promotion that required him to move to London for six months. It was an offer that they both knew he couldn't refuse. The salary was significant, and when he returned to New York in six months, he would be made a partner of the firm. Initially Lisa was very supportive, but as Brad's moving date neared, she became very clingy. She was no longer fine with Brad watching late-night TV in the living room; she wanted him to go to bed with her.

Brad indulged her needs and recognized that his move was going to be a difficult transition, particularly for Lisa. Lisa had lost her mother to cancer when she was ten years old, and her father had died in a drunk-driving accident when she was fourteen. Brad understood that Lisa had experienced a tremendous amount of loss, and he had reassured her in the past whenever she had become anxious and sad. But he was not prepared for Lisa's behavior after his move to London.

During her initial international phone calls to Brad, Lisa would cry and tell him how much she missed him. Brad missed Lisa too. Within a week Lisa was calling Brad eight times a day. His new position was intense and challenging, and his days were filled with meetings. Though Brad wasn't able to answer all of Lisa's phone calls, he made sure that his assistant, Linda, called Lisa back to explain that he was in a meeting and would return her call when he had a break. By the time he called her back, Lisa was filled with anger, which was quickly complicated by her jealous accusations about Brad and Linda. Brad had a difficult time consoling her over the telephone and found that his reassurances were increasingly met with more anger. He was feeling defeated by Lisa's anger and jealousy. With Brad apart from her, Lisa was in the grips of her abandonment schema.

Critical Partner Schema: Emotional Deprivation

The core emotions of the critical partner with an emotional deprivation schema are loneliness, bitterness, disappointment, and depression. Their worldview is that others will never meet their needs. The coping behavior of critical partners who overcompensate for a deprivation schema is to demand that all of their needs be provided for, which can result in their becoming overly demanding and angry when their emotional needs are not met (Young 2004).

♥ Alice and Neal's Story

Alice and Neal met on a matchmaking website when they were both in their fifties. Neal loved to woo women with his charming and witty e-mails. Alice appreciated his sense of humor and was looking forward to their first date. They shared an enjoyable conversation-filled evening together at an Italian restaurant. Their date concluded with a plan to get together the next day for a hike. Alice went to bed excited that the date had gone so well. She found Neal attractive and interesting. Their hike the next morning turned into lunch, followed by a movie. Alice and Neal were having a wonderful time together. Alice laughed at Neal's jokes, asked him questions that indicated how very interested she was in him, and was appropriately affectionate. When they said good-bye that evening, Neal suggested that they attend a jazz concert the next evening. Alice explained that she would love to go, but her work schedule as a flight attendant required her to fly to London the next day for two days. Neal said that he understood, and they agreed that they would talk when Alice returned and make plans at that time.

Neal went home that night feeling lonely and depressed. His increasingly loving feelings toward Alice triggered memories of the lack of love that he had experienced in his childhood. Neal grew up with two alcoholic parents who cared more about each other and their next drink than they cared about Neal. He was often dropped off at the apartment of an older lady who lived next door.

Though Neal experienced great chemistry with Alice, he had a rising anxiety that she would be unable to meet his needs. How could someone who made her living flying around the world take care of him? Two days later, when Alice got home, she was excited that she had a message on her phone from Neal. Jet-lagged, she returned his call just after taking a bath and a nap, but he seemed disappointed that she had waited to call him. They made arrangements to go out for dinner the next evening. After dating for three months, they realized that their relationship had progressed to the point where they could make the decision to live together. Alice owned her condo and Neal was renting his apartment, so they decided that they would make some modifications to her condo to give him a space for his work as a freelance consultant.

As Neal's move-in date neared, he was increasingly irritated with Alice. He would become angry and demanding when she didn't immediately accommodate his requests. Though Alice was committed to making the relationship work, she felt like a disappointment to Neal. The core problem was that the relationship made Neal vulnerable to his deprivation schema, and he coped with his vulnerable feelings by making angry demands.

Summary

This chapter presented the five primary critical partner schemas and their corresponding core emotions, worldviews, and coping behaviors. The stories about critical partners are not designed to illuminate all of the experiences that you might have with your partner, but to highlight some of the challenges others have experienced with each partner profile. Chapter 2 will provide the assessment tools necessary for you to identify your critical partner's schema. This process is the next step in providing you with an understanding of the core belief that drives your partner's emotional life.

Critical Partner Schemas

Defectiveness and Shame

- *Core emotions:* Shame and fear.
- *Worldview:* Sees self as bad, unwanted, inferior, or invalid in important respects, or fears becoming unlovable to a partner if her true self were exposed.
- *Behavior toward partner:* Critical, acts superior, presents as perfect, or some combination.

Entitlement

- *Core emotion:* Anger.
- *Worldview:* Feels superior to others and deserving of special treatment.
- *Behavior toward partner:* Controlling, manipulative, and selfish.

Mistrust and Abuse

- *Core emotions:* Fear and anxiety.
- *Worldview:* Feels that people cannot be trusted.

- *Behavior toward partner:* Can be abusive as a way to reassert control and protect self from hurt.

Abandonment

- *Core emotions:* Anxiety, sadness, depression, and anger.
- *Worldview:* Fears that important people will leave, behave unpredictably, or get sick and die.
- *Behavior toward partner:* Clingy, jealous and possessive, attacking, withdrawn, and controlling.

Emotional Deprivation

- *Core emotions:* Loneliness, bitterness, disappointment, and depression.
- *Worldview:* Feels that others will never meet his needs.
- *Behavior toward partner:* Demands that all her needs be met and becomes overly demanding and angry when her emotional needs are not met.

Chapter 2

Identifying Your Partner's Schema

This chapter will provide you with the tools you need to identify your critical partner's schema. As you work through the process of writing your partner's childhood history and filling out the worksheets with information based on his childhood experiences, you may find yourself viewing your partner a bit differently. When dealing with a critical partner, it is common to completely miss or lose sight of the fact that she was a child who had experiences that played a part in forming her behavior, her way of interacting with others, and her worldview.

Think about your partner's early childhood to adulthood. You will do your partner's assessment based on your current experience with him and your knowledge about his early childhood and adolescent years. Before you proceed with your partner's assessment, fill out the childhood history form (which follows). Write down as many descriptive words or phrases for each of your partner's family members as possible. The more that you can write, the more helpful it will be for you when you rate the statements in later worksheets on behalf of your partner. Include any significant experiences that you believe may have had a negative impact on your partner.

Additionally, write down any experiences that your partner has shared about interactions with peers during school. This will take some serious thought on your part, and you may need to engage your detective skills in order to respond to the statements accurately. For example, partners who have a defectiveness and shame schema often go to great lengths to hide their feelings of shame about their defectiveness. It may take some investigating to get to the truth about your partner's core beliefs and emotions. Remember Beth and Joe from chapter 1? Joe may never have told Beth that he felt shame about his father's cross-dressing and subsequent sex change, but he may have mentioned that he never had friends over to his home or even that he never had any close friends while growing up.

Once you have finished writing down descriptions of your partner's family and significant experiences during childhood and adolescence, you are ready to proceed to the worksheets. Be sure to keep what you've written close by, in case you need to refer to it during the assessment process.

Your Partner's Childhood History

Mother:

_____

_____

_____

_____

_____

Father:

_____

_____

_____

_____

_____

Siblings:

_____

_____

_____

_____

Peers:

_____

_____

_____

_____

Experiences:

_____

_____

_____

_____

If you feel that you have a good sense of your partner's schema from the information given in chapter 1, skip to the partner schema that you have identified and complete the worksheets associated with that schema. If you are confused or feel that more than one schema might fit your partner, then complete the worksheets under each of the five types of critical partners. [Note that the rating system may be slightly different with each worksheet, so please read the rating scale and interpretation carefully for each schema.]

Critical Partner Schema: Defectiveness and Shame

The following is the partner's childhood history form that Beth filled out for Joe. Later you'll find two worksheets that Beth completed as part of Joe's assessment.

Joe's Childhood History

Mother:

Kicked him out of the house.

Preferred her daughter to Joe.

Father:

Wore women's clothing.

Had sex change and now lives as a woman.

Siblings:

One younger sister, who was the favorite.

Never had a close relationship with his sister.

Peers:

Has never spoken of any close friends.

Is not in touch with any friends from childhood.

Experiences:

Was left at day care until 8:00 p.m. _____

Was occasionally forgotten at day care. _____

Parents divorced when he was seven years old. _____

Seemed to lack any type of support system. _____

Worksheet 2.1: Is Your Partner's Early Maladaptive Schema Defectiveness and Shame?

Adapted from the Young Schema Questionnaire with the permission and assistance of Jeffrey Young, Ph.D., the following statements are designed to identify a person's early maladaptive schema. Now, think about your partner and try to get into her mind. It is important that you stay focused on responding to the statements as you think your partner would, and avoid getting distracted by your thoughts about how the statements might relate to you. Try to rate the following statements as your partner would if he were responding from an honest and undefended place. Keep your partner's childhood history form close by, in case you need to refer to it.

Rating Scale

1 = completely untrue

2 = mostly untrue

3 = slightly more true than untrue

4 = moderately true

5 = mostly true

6 = absolutely true

Statement	Rating
1. Someone who really knew me couldn't love me.	
2. Because I am inherently flawed and defective, I am not worthy of love.	
3. I have secrets that I will not share, even with the people closest to me.	
4. I am to blame for my parents' inability to love me.	
5. I present a false self that hides the real me because the real me is unacceptable.	
6. I tend to be drawn to people who are critical and rejecting of me.	
7. I tend to be critical and rejecting of others, especially those who seem to love me.	
8. I tend to devalue my positive qualities.	
9. I feel a lot of shame about myself.	
10. Exposure of my faults is one of my greatest fears.	
Total: _____	

Interpreting Your Ratings

10–19   Very low. This schema probably does not apply to your partner.

20–29   Fairly low. This schema may only apply occasionally.

30–39   Moderate. This schema is an issue in your partner's life.

40–49   High. This is definitely an important schema for your partner.

50–60   Very high. This is definitely one of your partner's core schemas.

If you rated any statements as 5 or 6, this schema may still apply to your partner, even if the total is in the low range.

Beth filled out the worksheet as follows to determine Joe's early maladaptive schema.

Sample Worksheet 2.1: Beth's Ratings on Whether Joe's Early Maladaptive Schema Is Defectiveness and Shame

Statement	Rating
1. Someone who really knew me couldn't love me.	5
2. Because I am inherently flawed and defective, I am not worthy of love.	4
3. I have secrets that I will not share, even with the people closest to me.	6
4. I am to blame for my parents' inability to love me.	5
5. I present a false self that hides the real me because the real me is unacceptable.	5
6. I tend to be drawn to people who are critical and rejecting of me.	2
7. I tend to be critical and rejecting of others, especially those who seem to love me.	5
8. I tend to devalue my positive qualities.	2
9. I feel a lot of shame about myself.	4
10. Exposure of my faults is one of my greatest fears.	6
Total:	44

Beth rated each statement based on what she knows about Joe and his family experience. She gave four statements a rating of 5 and two statements a rating of 6. Based on these ratings and a total rating of 44, she determined that Joe has a defectiveness and shame schema.

Worksheet 2.2: Uncover the Origin of Your Partner's Defectiveness and Shame Schema

Adapted from the Young Schema Questionnaire with the permission and assistance of Jeffrey Young, Ph.D., the following statements are helpful in identifying the origins of your partner's early maladaptive schema. Thinking about your partner's mother and father, or primary caregiver in the absence of her mother and father, fill out the worksheet as if you were your partner. Rate the following statements as accurately as possible based on your knowledge of your partner's childhood. Refer to your partner's childhood history form if you feel stuck.

Rating Scale

1 = completely untrue

2 = mostly untrue

3 = slightly more true than untrue

4 = moderately true

5 = mostly true

6 = absolutely true

Identifying Your Partner's Schema

Statement	Mother	Father
1. My mother/father was extremely critical, demeaning, or punitive toward me.		
2. My mother/father repeatedly criticized or punished me for my appearance, behavior, or things I said.		
3. My mother/father rejected me or made me feel unloved as a child.		
4. My mother/father abused me sexually, physically, or emotionally when I was a child.		
5. My mother/father regularly blamed me when things went wrong in our family.		
6. My mother/father told me repeatedly that I was bad, worthless, or good-for-nothing.		
7. My mother/father repeatedly compared me in an unfavorable way to my sibling(s).		
8. My mother/father left home when I was a child, and I blamed myself.		
9. My mother/father made me feel ashamed of myself or her/him.		

Ratings: If you noted 4, 5, or 6 for any of the statements, add up how many times you wrote each of these ratings for your partner's mother and father. The greater the number of these higher ratings, the more likely it is that you've identified the source of this early maladaptive schema.

	4	5	6
Mother			
Father			

Interpreting Your Ratings

If you gave your partner's mother or father a rating of 4, 5, or 6 on one or more of the statements, it is likely that you have identified the origin of this early maladaptive schema for your partner.

Beth filled out the following worksheet to determine the origin of Joe's defectiveness and shame schema.

Sample Worksheet 2.2: Beth's Ratings on the Origin of Joe's Defectiveness and Shame Schema

Statement	Mother	Father
1. My mother/father was extremely critical, demeaning, or punitive toward me.	3	2
2. My mother/father repeatedly criticized or punished me for my appearance, behavior, or things I said.	3	2
3. My mother/father rejected me or made me feel unloved as a child.	5	3
4. My mother/father abused me sexually, physically, or emotionally when I was a child.	1	1
5. My mother/father regularly blamed me when things went wrong in our family.	5	2
6. My mother/father told me repeatedly that I was bad, worthless, or good-for-nothing.	4	2
7. My mother/father repeatedly compared me in an unfavorable way to my sibling(s).	6	2

8. My mother/father left home when I was a child, and I blamed myself.	*1*	3
9. My mother/father made me feel ashamed of myself or her/him.	3	6

Ratings: If you noted 4, 5, or 6 for any of the statements, add up how many times you wrote each of these ratings for your partner's mother and father.

	4	5	6
Mother	*1*	*2*	*1*
Father	0	0	*1*

Using this worksheet, Beth identified the origin of Joe's early maladaptive schema. Based on her ratings of the statements concerning Joe's parents, it appears that Joe's defectiveness and shame schema comes from his mother and father. While Beth found only one high rating for the statements about Joe's father, it is significant enough to confirm that his father and his mother, who has high ratings for four of the statements, are responsible for Joe's schema.

Critical Partner Schema: Entitlement

The following is the partner's childhood history form that Camille filled out for Tom. Later you'll find two worksheets that Camille completed as part of Tom's assessment.

Tom's Childhood History

Mother:

Extremely attentive.

Indulgent.

Her world revolved around her son.

Seems to put her needs second to her son's needs.

Father:

High standards but supportive.

Told Tom that he was the best and could do whatever he set his mind to.

Told Tom that he should never settle for less than the best.

Siblings:

Only child.

Peers:

Very social.

Lots of friends.

Tom is definitely the leader of the pack with his friends.

Experiences:

Parents always objected if they felt Tom wasn't getting the best—the best lacrosse coach, the best English teacher, the best cashmere sweater—because Tom deserved the best.

Worksheet 2.3: Is Your Partner's Early Maladaptive Schema Entitlement?

Adapted from the Young Schema Questionnaire with the permission and assistance of Jeffrey Young, Ph.D., the following statements are designed to identify your partner's early maladaptive schema. Now, think about your partner and try to get into his mind. It is important that you stay focused on responding to the statements as you think your partner would, and avoid getting distracted by your thoughts about how the statements might relate to you. Try to rate the following statements as your partner would if she were responding from an honest and undefended place. Keep your partner's childhood history form close by, in case you need to refer to it.

Rating Scale

1 = completely untrue

2 = mostly untrue

3 = slightly more true than untrue

4 = moderately true

5 = mostly true

6 = absolutely true

Statement	Rating
1. No is an answer that I have trouble accepting.	
2. When I don't get what I want, I get angry.	
3. I am special and should not have to accept, or be held to, normal restrictions.	
4. I always put my needs first.	
5. I have a very difficult time getting myself to stop drinking, smoking, overeating, or engaging in other problematic behaviors.	
6. I lack discipline when it comes to completing routine or boring tasks.	
7. I act on impulses and emotions, and this results in consequences.	
8. When I cannot reach a goal, I become frustrated and give up.	
9. I insist that things get done my way.	
10. My need for immediate gratification can get in the way of my reaching a long-term goal.	
Total: _____	

Interpreting Your Ratings

10–19 Very low. This schema probably does not apply to your partner.

20–29 Fairly low. This schema may only apply occasionally.

30–39 Moderate. This schema is an issue in your partner's life.

40–49 High. This is definitely an important schema for your partner.

50–60 Very high. This is definitely one of your partner's core schemas.

If you rated any statements as 5 or 6, this schema may still apply to your partner, even if the total is in the low range.

Camille filled out the following worksheet to uncover Tom's early maladaptive schema.

Sample Worksheet 2.3: Camille's Ratings on Whether Tom's Early Maladaptive Schema Is Entitlement

Statement	Rating
1. No is an answer that I have trouble accepting.	6
2. When I don't get what I want, I get angry.	6
3. I am special and should not have to accept, or be held to, normal restrictions.	6
4. I always put my needs first.	6

5. I have a very difficult time getting myself to stop drinking, smoking, overeating, or engaging in other problematic behaviors.	3
6. I lack discipline when it comes to completing routine or boring tasks.	3
7. I act on impulses and emotions, and this results in consequences.	3
8. When I cannot reach a goal, I become frustrated and give up.	3
9. I insist that things get done my way.	5
10. My need for immediate gratification can get in the way of my reaching a long-term goal.	4
Total: __45__	

Camille rated each statement based on what she knew about Tom and his family experience. She gave one statement a rating of 5 and four statements a rating of 6. Based on these ratings and a total of 45, Camille determined that Tom has an entitlement schema.

Worksheet 2.4: Uncover the Origin of Your Partner's Entitlement Schema

Adapted from the Young Schema Questionnaire with the permission and assistance of Jeffrey Young, Ph.D., the following statements are helpful in identifying the origins of your partner's early maladaptive schema. Thinking about your partner's mother and father, or primary caregiver in the absence of his mother and father, fill out the worksheet as if you were your partner. Rate the following statements as accurately as possible based on your knowledge of your partner's childhood. Refer to your partner's childhood history form if you feel stuck.

Rating Scale

1 = completely untrue

2 = mostly untrue

3 = slightly more true than untrue

4 = moderately true

5 = mostly true

6 = absolutely true

Statement	Mother	Father
1. My mother/father spoiled me.		
2. My mother/father was overindulgent with me in many areas.		
3. My mother/father told me or made me feel that I was very special.		
4. My mother/father told me or made me feel that I was better than other people.		
5. My mother/father was demanding and expected everything to get done her/his way.		
6. My mother/father didn't teach me that the needs of others are as important as mine.		

Ratings: If you noted 4, 5, or 6 for any of the statements, add up how many times you wrote each of these ratings for your partner's mother and father.

	4	5	6
Mother			
Father			

Interpreting Your Ratings

If you gave your partner's mother or father a rating of 4, 5, or 6 on one or more of the statements, it is likely that you have identified the origin of this early maladaptive schema for your partner.

Camille filled out the following worksheet to uncover the origin of Tom's entitlement schema.

Sample Worksheet 2.4: Camille's Ratings on the Origin of Tom's Entitlement Schema

Statement	Mother	Father
1. My mother/father spoiled me.	6	6
2. My mother/father was overindulgent with me in many areas.	5	5
3. My mother/father told me or made me feel that I was very special.	6	6
4. My mother/father told me or made me feel that I was better than other people.	5	5
5. My mother/father was demanding and expected everything to get done her/his way.	1	3
6. My mother/father didn't teach me that the needs of others are as important as mine.	5	5

Ratings: If you noted 4, 5, or 6 for any of the statements, add up how many times you wrote each of these ratings for your partner's mother and father.			
	4	5	6
Mother	0	3	2
Father	0	3	2

Using this worksheet, Camille identified the origin of Tom's early maladaptive schema. Camille gave three statements a rating of 5 and two statements a rating of 6 for each of Tom's parents. Tom's entitlement schema comes from his mother and father.

Critical Partner Schema: Mistrust and Abuse

The following is the partner's childhood history form that Ron filled out for Elizabeth. Later you'll find two worksheets that he completed as part of Elizabeth's assessment.

Elizabeth's Childhood History

Mother:

Inconsistent—very loving and then very critical.

If her husband criticized her, then she would criticize Elizabeth.

Father:

Drank every night after work.

Very angry when fueled with alcohol.

Would hit Elizabeth.

Was loving to Elizabeth when he was sober.

Siblings:

One older brother, moved in with his girlfriend's family when he was sixteen years old because he couldn't be around their dad.

Elizabeth spoke to her brother frequently for understanding and support about their parents.

Peers:

Had lots of friends, but she didn't share her family secrets or problems with any of them.

Didn't have friends to her home.

Experiences:

Dad came home drunk when Elizabeth was getting ready to leave for the prom; called her a slut, hit her, and tore her dress. She had to call her date and cancel their prom night.

Worksheet 2.5: Is Your Partner's Early Maladaptive Schema Mistrust and Abuse?

Adapted from the Young Schema Questionnaire with the permission and assistance of Jeffrey Young, Ph.D., the following statements are designed to identify your partner's early maladaptive schema. Now, think about your partner and try to get into her mind. It is important that you stay focused on responding to the statements as you think your partner would, and avoid getting distracted by your thoughts about how the statements might relate to you. Try to rate the following statements as your partner would if he were responding from an honest and undefended place. Keep your partner's childhood history form close by, in case you need to refer to it.

Rating Scale

1 = completely untrue

2 = mostly untrue

3 = slightly more true than untrue

4 = moderately true

5 = mostly true

6 = absolutely true

Statement	Rating
1. I have the expectation that people will hurt me or use me.	
2. People close to me have consistently abused me.	
3. I know that it is only a matter of time before the people who are important in my life betray me.	
4. I must protect myself and be on guard.	
5. People will take advantage of me if I am not careful.	
6. I regularly set up tests for people to determine if they are really on my side.	
7. I tend to hurt others before they can hurt me.	
8. I fear that people will hurt me if I allow them to get close to me.	
9. When I think about what people have done to me, I get angry.	
10. The people whom I should have been able to trust have physically, verbally, or sexually abused me.	
Total: _____	

Interpreting Your Ratings

10–19 Very low. This schema probably does not apply to your partner.

20–29 Fairly low. This schema may only apply occasionally.

30–39 Moderate. This schema is an issue in your partner's life.

40–49 High. This is definitely an important schema for your partner.

50–60 Very high. This is definitely one of your partner's core schemas.

If you rated any statements as 5 or 6, this schema may still apply to your partner, even if the total is in the low range.

Ron filled out the following worksheet to uncover Elizabeth's early maladaptive schema.

Sample Worksheet 2.5: Ron's Ratings on Whether Elizabeth's Early Maladaptive Schema Is Mistrust and Abuse

Statement	Rating
1. I have the expectation that people will hurt me or use me.	4
2. People close to me have consistently abused me.	6
3. I know that it is only a matter of time before the people who are important in my life betray me.	5

4. I must protect myself and be on guard.	5
5. People will take advantage of me if I am not careful.	4
6. I regularly set up tests for people to determine if they are really on my side.	4
7. I tend to hurt others before they can hurt me.	3
8. I fear that people will hurt me if I allow them to get close to me.	6
9. When I think about what people have done to me, I get angry.	3
10. The people whom I should have been able to trust have physically, verbally, or sexually abused me.	6
Total: ___46___	

Ron rated each statement based on what he knows about Elizabeth and her family experience. He gave two statements a rating of 5 and three statements a rating of 6. Based on these scores and a total of 46, he determined that Elizabeth has a mistrust and abuse schema.

Worksheet 2.6: Uncover the Origin of Your Partner's Mistrust and Abuse Schema

Adapted from the Young Schema Questionnaire with the permission and assistance of Jeffrey Young, Ph.D., the following statements can help you identify the origins of your partner's early maladaptive schema. Thinking about your partner's mother and father, or primary caregiver in the absence of her mother and father, fill out the worksheet as if you were your partner. Rate the following statements as accurately as possible based on your knowledge of your partner's childhood. Refer to your partner's childhood history form if you feel stuck.

Rating Scale

1 = completely untrue

2 = mostly untrue

3 = slightly more true than untrue

4 = moderately true

5 = mostly true

6 = absolutely true

Statement	Mother	Father
1. My mother/father physically abused me as a child.		
2. My mother/father sexually abused me or repeatedly touched me in a sexually provocative way when I was a child.		
3. My mother/father verbally or emotionally abused me, or both (for example, repeatedly humiliated me, teased me, or put me down).		
4. My mother/father seemed to take pleasure in seeing me suffer.		
5. My mother/father threatened me with severe punishment or retaliation to get me to do things.		
6. My mother/father regularly warned me not to trust people outside of our family.		
7. My mother/father made me feel that she/he was against me.		
8. My mother/father betrayed me in a way that made me feel that I couldn't trust her/him.		

Ratings: If you noted 4, 5, or 6 for any of the statements, add up how many times you wrote each of these ratings for your partner's mother and father.

	4	5	6
Mother			
Father			

Interpreting Your Ratings

If you gave your partner's mother or father a rating of 4, 5, or 6 on one or more of the statements, it is likely that you have identified the origin of this early maladaptive schema for your partner.

Ron filled out the following worksheet to uncover the origin of Elizabeth's mistrust and abuse schema.

Sample Worksheet 2.6: Ron's Ratings on the Origin of Elizabeth's Mistrust and Abuse Schema

Statement	Mother	Father
1. My mother/father physically abused me as a child.	1	6
2. My mother/father sexually abused me or repeatedly touched me in a sexually provocative way when I was a child.	1	1

3. My mother/father verbally or emotionally abused me, or both (for example, repeatedly humiliated me, teased me, or put me down).	6	5
4. My mother/father seemed to take pleasure in seeing me suffer.	4	4
5. My mother/father threatened me with severe punishment or retaliation to get me to do things.	3	5
6. My mother/father regularly warned me not to trust people outside of our family.	2	2
7. My mother/father made me feel that she/he was against me.	3	4
8. My mother/father betrayed me in a way that made me feel that I couldn't trust her/him.	3	3

Ratings: If you noted 4, 5, or 6 for any of the statements, add up how many times you wrote each of these ratings for your partner's mother and father.

	4	5	6
Mother	1	0	1
Father	2	2	1

Ron identified the origin of Elizabeth's early maladaptive schema as her mother and father. They would each only need one statement with a high rating to be identified as the origin, but Elizabeth's mother received two high ratings and her father received five.

Critical Partner Schema: Abandonment

The following is the partner's childhood history form that Brad filled out for Lisa. Later you'll find two worksheets that he completed as part of Lisa's assessment.

Lisa's Childhood History

Mother:

Had a close relationship.

Died of cancer when Lisa was ten years old.

Father:

Supportive and loving.

Died in a car accident when Lisa was fourteen years old.

Siblings:

One sister, four years older, who was a freshman in college when their dad died.

Peers:

Moved in with her best friend's family when her father died.

Very social—big network of friends.

Experiences:

Relationships with boyfriends in high school didn't last long. The boys ended them because they felt overwhelmed by Lisa's needs and her emotional state when they couldn't or wouldn't meet her needs.

Worksheet 2.7: Is Your Partner's Early Maladaptive Schema Abandonment?

Adapted from the Young Schema Questionnaire with the permission and assistance of Jeffrey Young, Ph.D., the following statements are designed to identify your partner's early maladaptive schema. Now, think about your partner and try to get into his mind. It is important that you stay focused on responding to the statements as you think your partner would, and avoid getting distracted by your thoughts about how the statements might relate to you. Try to rate the following statements as your partner would if she were responding from an honest and undefended place. Keep your partner's childhood history form close by, in case you need to refer to it.

Rating Scale

1 = completely untrue

2 = mostly untrue

3 = slightly more true than untrue

4 = moderately true

5 = mostly true

6 = absolutely true

Statement	Rating
1. I am fearful that people I love will die or leave me.	
2. I get clingy with people when I feel that they are going to leave me.	
3. My support system feels unstable.	
4. I find myself falling in love with people who aren't capable of committing to me or willing to do so.	
5. People have always moved in and out of my life.	

6. When someone I love pulls away, I feel desperate.	
7. My obsession with the idea that my lovers will leave me drives them away.	
8. The people with whom I have the closest relationships are unpredictable. Sometimes they are there for me, and sometimes they are not.	
9. I feel as if I need people more than others do.	
10. I feel as if I will be alone toward the end of my life.	
Total: _____	

Interpreting Your Ratings

10–19 Very low. This schema probably does not apply to your partner.

20–29 Fairly low. This schema may only apply occasionally.

30–39 Moderate. This schema is an issue in your partner's life.

40–49 High. This is definitely an important schema for your partner.

50–60 Very high. This is definitely one of your partner's core schemas.

If you rated any of the statements as 5 or 6, this schema may still apply to your partner, even if the total is in the low range.

Brad filled out the following worksheet to determine whether Lisa's early maladaptive schema was abandonment.

Sample Worksheet 2.7: Brad's Ratings on Whether Lisa's Early Maladaptive Schema Is Abandonment

Statement	Rating
1. I am fearful that people I love will die or leave me.	6
2. I get clingy with people when I feel that they are going to leave me.	6
3. My support system feels unstable.	2
4. I find myself falling in love with people who aren't capable of committing to me or willing to do so.	2
5. People have always moved in and out of my life.	2
6. When someone I love pulls away, I feel desperate.	5
7. My obsession with the idea that my lovers will leave me drives them away.	5
8. The people with whom I have the closest relationships are unpredictable. Sometimes they are there for me, and sometimes they are not.	2
9. I feel as if I need people more than others do.	4
10. I feel as if I will be alone toward the end of my life.	4
Total:	38

Brad gave two statements a rating of 5 and two statements a rating of 6. Based on these ratings and a total of 38, Brad determined that Lisa has an abandonment schema.

Worksheet 2.8: Uncover the Origin of Your Partner's Abandonment Schema

Adapted from the Young Schema Questionnaire with the permission and assistance of Jeffrey Young, Ph.D., the following statements will help you identify the origins of your partner's early maladaptive schema. Thinking about your partner's mother and father, or primary caregiver in the absence of his mother and father, fill out the worksheet as if you were your partner. Rate the following statements as accurately as possible based on your knowledge of your partner's childhood. Refer to your partner's childhood history form if you feel stuck.

Rating Scale

1 = completely untrue

2 = mostly untrue

3 = slightly more true than untrue

4 = moderately true

5 = mostly true

6 = absolutely true

Statement	Mother	Father
1. My mother/father died or left home when I was young.		
2. My mother/father preferred my sibling(s) to me.		
3. My mother/father was unstable.		
4. My mother/father suffered from depression and withdrew from me on a regular basis.		
5. My mother/father was unpredictable and withdrew from me on a regular basis.		

6. My mother/father was addicted to drugs, alcohol, or both, and would "check out" frequently.		

Ratings: If you noted 4, 5, or 6 for any of the statements, add up how many times you wrote each of these ratings for your partner's mother and father.

	4	5	6
Mother			
Father			

Interpreting Your Ratings

If you gave your partner's mother or father a rating of 4, 5, or 6 on one or more of the statements, it is likely that you have identified the origin of this early maladaptive schema for your partner.

Brad filled out the following worksheet to determine the origin of Lisa's abandonment schema.

Sample Worksheet 2.8: Brad's Ratings on the Origin of Lisa's Abandonment Schema

Statement	Mother	Father
1. My mother/father died or left home when I was young.	6	6
2. My mother/father preferred my sibling(s) to me.	1	1

3. My mother/father was unstable.	1	1
4. My mother/father suffered from depression and withdrew from me on a regular basis.	1	1
5. My mother/father was unpredictable and withdrew from me on a regular basis.	1	1
6. My mother/father was addicted to drugs, alcohol, or both, and would "check out" frequently.	1	1

Ratings: If you noted 4, 5, or 6 for any of the statements, add up how many times you wrote each of these ratings for your partner's mother and father.

	4	5	6
Mother	0	0	1
Father	0	0	1

Brad gave Lisa's mother and father each a rating of 6 on one of the statements. Both Lisa's mother and father are the origin of her abandonment schema.

Critical Partner Schema: Emotional Deprivation

The following is the partner's childhood history form that Alice filled out for Neal. Later you'll find two worksheets that she completed as part of Neal's assessment.

Neal's Childhood History

Mother:

An alcoholic.

Codependent with her husband.

Treated Neal as an afterthought.

Father:

An alcoholic.

Codependent with his wife.

Only activity with Neal was watching TV.

Siblings:

Only child.

Peers:

Had superficial relationships at school.

Parents had no connection to his school or his peers' parents, which isolated him, leaving him with no sense of community.

Experiences:

Neal's parents told him that because they were going out of town for the weekend, he would need to stay with the elderly lady who lived next door. During the two days and nights he stayed with the neighbor, Neal heard noises coming from his parents' apartment. Sadly, he realized his parents had stayed home the entire weekend.

Worksheet 2.9: Is Your Partner's Early Maladaptive Schema Emotional Deprivation?

Adapted from the Young Schema Questionnaire with the permission and assistance of Jeffrey Young, Ph.D., the following statements are designed to identify your partner's early maladaptive schema. Now, think about your partner and try to get into her mind. It is important that you stay focused on responding to the statements as you think your partner would, and avoid getting distracted by your thoughts about how the statements might relate to you. Try to rate the following statements as your partner would if he were responding from an honest and undefended place. Keep your partner's childhood history form close by, in case you need to refer to it.

Rating Scale

1 = completely untrue

2 = mostly untrue

3 = slightly more true than untrue

4 = moderately true

5 = mostly true

6 = absolutely true

Statement	Rating
1. I don't get as much love as I need.	
2. I feel as if no one really understands me.	
3. I am usually attracted to cold partners who can't meet my needs.	
4. I don't feel connected, even to the people who are closest to me.	

5. I have not had one special person in my life who wants to share himself/ herself with me and cares about what happens to me.	
6. I don't have anyone in my life to hold me or give me warmth and affection.	
7. I do not have a person in my life who really listens and is tuned in to my true needs and feelings.	
8. I find it difficult to let people guide or protect me, even though it is what I want.	
9. I find it difficult to let people love me.	
10. I feel lonely most of the time.	
	Total: _____

Interpreting Your Ratings

10–19 Very low. This schema probably does not apply to your partner.

20–29 Fairly low. This schema may only apply occasionally.

30–39 Moderate. This schema is an issue in your partner's life.

40–49 High. This is definitely an important schema for your partner.

50–60 Very high. This is definitely one of your partner's core schemas.

If you rated any of the statements as 5 or 6, this schema may still apply to your partner, even if the total is in the low range.

Alice filled out the following worksheet to determine Neal's early maladaptive schema.

The Critical Partner

Sample Worksheet 2.9: Alice's Ratings on Whether Neal's Early Maladaptive Schema Is Emotional Deprivation

Statement	Rating
1. I don't get as much love as I need.	6
2. I feel as if no one really understands me.	5
3. I am usually attracted to cold partners who can't meet my needs.	4
4. I don't feel connected, even to the people who are closest to me.	4
5. I have not had one special person in my life who wants to share himself/herself with me and cares about what happens to me.	4
6. I don't have anyone in my life to hold me or give me warmth and affection.	4
7. I do not have a person in my life who really listens and is tuned in to my true needs and feelings.	3
8. I find it difficult to let people guide or protect me, even though it is what I want.	5
9. I find it difficult to let people love me.	6
10. I feel lonely most of the time.	4
Total:	45

Alice rated each statement based on what she knows about Neal and his family experience. Alice gave two statements a rating of 5 and two statements a rating of 6. Based on these ratings and a total of 45, Alice determined that Neal has an emotional deprivation schema.

50

Worksheet 2.10: Uncover the Origin of Your Partner's Emotional Deprivation Schema

Adapted from the Young Schema Questionnaire with the permission and assistance of Jeffrey Young, Ph.D., the following statements can help identify the origins of your partner's early maladaptive schema. Thinking about your partner's mother and father, or primary caregiver in the absence of her mother and father, fill out the worksheet as if you were your partner. Rate the following statements as accurately as possible based on your knowledge of your partner's childhood. Refer to your partner's childhood history form if you feel stuck.

Rating Scale

1 = completely untrue

2 = mostly untrue

3 = slightly more true than untrue

4 = moderately true

5 = mostly true

6 = absolutely true

Statement	Mother	Father
1. My mother/father was cold and unaffectionate with me when I was a child.		
2. My mother/father did not make me feel loved and valued. She/he did not make me feel special.		
3. My mother/father did not give me adequate time and attention.		
4. My mother/father was not tuned in to my needs when I was a child.		

5. My mother/father did not give me adequate guidance when I was a child.		
6. My mother/father was not solid enough for me to feel that I could rely on her/him.		

Ratings: If you noted 4, 5, or 6 for any of the statements, add up how many times you wrote each of these ratings for your partner's mother and father.

	4	5	6
Mother			
Father			

Interpreting Your Ratings

If you gave your partner's mother or father a rating of 4, 5, or 6 on one of more of the statements, it is likely that you have identified the origin of this early maladaptive schema for your partner.

Alice filled out the following worksheet to determine the origin of Neal's emotional deprivation schema.

Sample Worksheet 2.10: Alice's Ratings on the Origin of Neal's Emotional Deprivation Schema

Statement	Mother	Father
1. My mother/father was cold and unaffectionate with me when I was a child.	5	5
2. My mother/father did not make me feel loved and valued. She/he did not make me feel special.	6	6
3. My mother/father did not give me adequate time and attention.	6	5
4. My mother/father was not tuned in to my needs when I was a child.	5	5
5. My mother/father did not give me adequate guidance when I was a child.	6	6
6. My mother/father was not solid enough for me to feel that I could rely on her/him.	5	5

Ratings: If you noted 4, 5, or 6 for any of the statements, add up how many times you wrote each of these ratings for your partner's mother and father.

	4	5	6
Mother	0	3	3
Father	0	4	2

Using this worksheet, Alice identified the origin of Neal's early maladaptive schema as his mother and his father. Alice gave three ratings of 5 and three rating of 6 for Neal's mother, and four ratings of 5 and two ratings of 6 for his father. His parents are responsible for his schema.

Summary

As you went through the process of writing out your partner's childhood history and rating the statements on the two worksheets for your partner, you may have found yourself developing more empathy for him as you came to understand the pain that he experienced during childhood. This helps to eliminate having a one-dimensional portrait of your partner as "the critic." You may now have a better understanding of why your partner is critical. Incorporating the portrait of your partner as a child experiencing the hurt that contributed to developing her schema into your more familiar picture of your adult partner creates a multidimensional profile that allows for greater understanding and communication. When you begin to work with the alternative coping strategies in chapters 6 and 7, you will find that the insight you have gained about your partner will be helpful as you begin to make necessary changes in your relationship.

Chapter 3

What Makes You Vulnerable to Criticism?

Now that you have determined your partner's schema, the next step is to understand more about yourself and what makes you vulnerable to criticism. Five schemas have been identified as making a person vulnerable to choosing a critical partner and vulnerable to what the critical partner says and does. It is important to note that four of the five schemas are the same as the ones that have been identified for critical partners. Don't be confused by this similarity. Keep in mind that a schema is the core belief that a person develops when one or more of his core needs are not met during childhood and adolescence. Different behaviors can be driven by the same schema, which can make two people with the same schema look quite different. The details about how these differences come about will be discussed in chapter 5, when we examine schema coping behaviors, schema maintenance, and schema magnets.

Additionally, it is important to note that while the schema is the core belief, the behaviors driven by the schema are separate from the schema itself. As mentioned, the specific coping behaviors for each schema can make two people with the same schema appear to be quite different. The critical partner's specific coping behavior is overcompensation, which makes that person critical. The vulnerable partner's coping behavior is to surrender, which makes you vulnerable to criticism. Chapter 5 will explain this further, but it is important to keep the basic concept in mind when you fill out the worksheets to identify your schema and determine its origin.

The stories associated with each of the five schemas paint a picture of the person's childhood experiences, the schema that was formed by the childhood experiences, and the enduring pattern of the core belief. The stories illustrate the way in which our core beliefs direct how we live our lives, our partner choices, and our emotional reactions to situations.

Vulnerable Partner Schema: Subjugation

The core emotions of vulnerable partners with a subjugation schema are fear, anxiety, and depression. The core behavior of these people is that they take care of other people before they take care of themselves, and they allow themselves to be controlled by their partners or significant others. Their worldview is that the needs and wants of others come before their own needs and wants, they matter less than others do, and it is bad for them to have their own needs and desires. People who are driven by this schema are drawn to dominant, controlling partners—and they are compliant.

♥ Susan's Story

Susan grew up in a household with a father who was the chief of surgery at a leading hospital, a mother who was the perfect wife to her very busy and successful husband, and three older brothers who, among the three of them, excelled at every sport imaginable. Susan was an attractive girl who was successful in school and well liked by her peers. Having grown up playing tennis, she was on the tennis team in high school. She would have preferred swimming, but when she voiced her preference to her parents, they made it very clear that tennis would be her sport—end of discussion. Susan's parents always seemed to be in agreement.

As Susan got older, she realized that this was because her mother agreed with and supported whatever Susan's father wanted. Her mom was also very accommodating to Susan's three older brothers. In fact, the world seemed to revolve around the male figures in the family. Susan's father and brothers always dominated the dinner-table conversation. Susan was never asked her opinion about any subject that was being discussed. In fact, she remembers that when she was addressed by anyone at the table, it was usually a request for her to get more milk or water for her brothers. Susan grew up feeling that her needs mattered less than those of the other members of her family and that she should take care of others before she took care of herself. Susan's childhood experiences would make her vulnerable in her adult life to relationships, situations, and behavior that triggered her subjugation schema.

As college neared, Susan was seriously considering becoming a medical doctor. She had a lot of respect for her father and loved to help people. When she mentioned her desire to her parents, her father insisted (and her mother agreed) that nursing would be a more suitable profession for her because of her gender and her future role as a wife and mother. Her father wondered aloud why they would invest all of the money in a medical school degree when she would probably quit working once she got married, or certainly when she had her first child. Susan's first emotion was disappointment, which was quickly replaced by a feeling of certainty that her father was right.

Susan finished nursing school and, as her parents had hoped, met a bright, young, hard-driving resident named Kirk. It made sense to Susan that she needed to make her schedule accommodate Kirk's schedule, because he was a doctor and she was "just" a nurse. Her friends frequently told her that she didn't need to switch her shifts to match his, but she insisted that he really needed to have her available on his days off so that she could take care of him, · because a resident's life is very demanding and stressful. What she didn't tell her friends was that when she couldn't switch her schedule to match Kirk's, he would become upset and criticize her for being unable to accomplish the simplest task. Kirk would say, "Jesus, Susan, you know how crushing the demands are on me and the dozens of life-and-death situations that I deal with daily, and you can't pull off switching your schedule to make my life a little easier!" It hurt Susan's feelings when he yelled at her and made her feel "less than," but he had a valid point, so she put him first.

Vulnerable Partner Schema: Defectiveness and Shame

The core emotions of vulnerable partners with a defectiveness and shame schema are shame and fear. These people's core behaviors are that they are self-conscious and compare themselves to others. Their worldview is that they are defective, bad, unwanted, inferior, or invalid. The coping behaviors associated with someone who is surrendering to this schema are to choose critical partners and to be self-critical as well.

In the discussion about this schema in chapter 1, the same schema for the critical partner looks different because the critical partner's behavior is overcompensation.

♥ Rachel's Story

Rachel's mother and father were each of their families' only children. Rachel, her parents' first baby, was born six weeks premature. Her parents' lack of experience, coupled with the additional responsibilities of caring for a premature infant, made for a very stressful environment.

Rachel was a "colicky" baby who cried frequently and was inconsolable. When her parents tried to comfort her and she continued to cry, they felt incompetent and frustrated. At first, they blamed themselves and their lack of experience with infants. At times of intense frustration, they reasoned that Rachel might be better off left alone in her crib to practice self-soothing, since their efforts were unsuccessful. So they left their infant in her crib to cry, closed the door to her room, and went downstairs to the TV room to watch a movie and take a much-needed break from Rachel's crying. This became a regular coping strategy for her parents.

When Rachel was two years old, her mom unexpectedly became pregnant. Her parents were still experiencing life with her as stressful and frustrating, so they briefly considered terminating the pregnancy. Ultimately, they decided against it and felt that they had made the correct decision when they were rewarded with a full-term, beautiful, and happy baby girl. They were so happy that they could not help but comment frequently on the marked contrast between defective Rachel and perfect Charlotte. Charlotte's happy disposition was rewarded with the constant attention of her parents. Rachel was often told to go play in her room by herself while her mom and dad focused their attention on Charlotte.

Her parents' experience with Charlotte convinced them that they weren't bad parents. In fact, they believed that Rachel had been the problem. This was the message that Rachel received from her parents throughout her childhood. If Rachel had a problem, it was a problem because of Rachel. She was made to feel defective. Her childhood history makes Rachel vulnerable to situations and behaviors that trigger her defectiveness and shame schema.

As an adult, Rachel was an attractive woman who seemed oblivious to her outward appearance. She was a popular draw for men, some of whom were too shy or insecure to approach her because they thought she was probably out of their league. The equally attractive "nice" guys were attracted to her, made an effort with compliments, and behaved well, but she was suspicious of them. She couldn't believe what they told her: how attractive she was, that they wanted to go out with her, that they liked her. If she didn't dump them first, they would usually grow weary of having their thoughtful comments and efforts squashed. A typical exchange would start with "Rachel, you look pretty tonight," to which Rachel would reply, "No I don't. I have a pimple on my chin, and I think I look fat in these jeans." How was a guy supposed to respond to that? It was too much work for most guys. Unfortunately, the guys who were successful with Rachel were often critical and tended to withhold compliments. Rachel found it easy to believe them.

Rachel fell hard for Chris. She knew that she didn't deserve him and worried constantly that he would figure out that he could have someone better. Chris played into Rachel's insecurity by always commenting on attractive women. When he had too much to drink, he would make unkind comparisons between Rachel and other attractive women. It was painfully similar to what she experienced with her parents and their constant comparisons of her and Charlotte. Rachel became so accustomed to the unkind comparisons that when others weren't making them, she would make them herself.

Vulnerable Partner Schema: Mistrust and Abuse

The core emotions of vulnerable partners with a mistrust and abuse schema are fear and anxiety. These people's core behavior is to be guarded and suspicious, and their worldview is that people cannot be trusted. The coping behavior of people who surrender to this schema is to choose unpredictable and untrustworthy partners. While it seems paradoxical that someone who believes that people can't be trusted would make the unconscious choice of an untrustworthy partner, it serves to reinforce what the vulnerable partner believes to be true.

In the discussion about this schema in chapter 1, it looks different in the critical partner because the critical partner's behavior is overcompensation.

♥ Julie's Story

Julie and her twin brother, John, grew up in a lively and dramatic show-business home in the Bel Air section of Los Angeles. Their father was a director, their mother was an actor, and both parents were recognizable public figures. Their home was always filled with Hollywood people. Their parents were notorious for their all-night parties, and when Julie and John went to bed at night they never knew whom they would wake up to in the morning. It was the 1970s, and "swinging" was a popular term and practice among this group, although Julie and John were too young to understand what it meant.

When Julie was twelve years old, she became more aware of some of the risqué activities taking place in their home. One incident would eclipse all others and be forever locked in her mind. Her father was in London directing a movie for three months, and her mother was at home in Los Angeles filming on a Hollywood set. The regular Hollywood parties continued at their home during their father's absence. But one Saturday morning, everything changed when Julie arrived home unexpectedly early from a sleepover at a friend's home the previous night. Julie sneaked in the kitchen door in an effort to avoid waking up her mother and any of her friends who had slept over. As Julie tiptoed by her parents' bedroom, she peeked into the room and saw a naked man walking from the bathroom back to the bed. She averted her eyes and then heard her mother's voice: "James, come back to bed.

I missed you." Julie was stunned. James? Uncle James? James had been considered part of their family from the time she and John were born. She gasped and her mother and Uncle James turned and saw her standing by the door.

From that fateful moment on, Julie felt as though she was on a roller coaster that seemed as if it might fly off the tracks at any moment. Some of the details escaped her memory, but monumental events followed. Her father returned from England and then moved out of their home. Her mother confessed that James was Julie and John's biological father, and both children were shipped off to boarding school in an effort to protect them from the scandal. Julie would never forget how her mother had deceived and betrayed her. If she couldn't trust her mother, whom could she trust? This childhood experience makes Julie vulnerable to behaviors and situations that trigger her mistrust and abuse schema.

By the time Julie started college, the searing pain of her mother's betrayal had been replaced by a dull but constant ache. It haunted her that she could have been so close to her mother and not known that her mother was hiding something so monumental. How had the man who she'd thought was her biological father not figured out the secret that his wife had kept from him? How much longer would it have gone on if Julie hadn't accidentally stumbled upon her mother and Uncle James? *Things are never as they appear. Everyone could be hiding a big secret, something potentially hurtful to people close to them.* These thoughts raced through Julie's mind every time she met someone. Julie believed that no one could be trusted.

Julie's choice of men became predictable: the guys who came in the "nice" package—the ones who called her when they said they would, treated her well, and included her in their plans with friends—were the ones that made her the most suspicious. Julie thought, *Guys like that must be hiding something, because they just seem too good to be true.* These guys were tossed aside for guys who were unpredictable and untrustworthy. Ken was not the guy that any of Julie's sorority sisters would have picked for her. He was handsome, but with an edge that gave him a "bad boy" vibe. Julie and Ken met at an after-hours bar that Julie and her friends went to after a long night of drinking. When Julie's eyes locked with Ken's, she knew that she would go home with him—and she did. The next day, when she was back in her room at her sorority house, she felt a bit ashamed about her promiscuous behavior under the influence of lots of cocktails, but her overwhelming feeling was excitement about having met Ken and seeing him again. Ken told her that he would call her the next day because they had discussed doing something the following night.

But excitement turned to disappointment over the next three days as she waited for him to call. When he finally called, he sounded upbeat and was ready to get together. Julie's first comment was to point out that she had expected to see him days ago, as they had discussed. Ken retorted, "Whoa babe, if you're going to be a nag, then I'm not interested. I got a lot going on. I can't be with a chick who needs me to hold her hand all of the time. Do you want to go out again or not?" Julie quickly replied, "Yes, I want to see you again." She always had a blast when she was with him, but she rarely knew when she was going to see him again. On the occasions when Julie would ask questions or complain, Ken would get defensive and sometimes angry and critical toward her.

Vulnerable Partner Schema: Emotional Deprivation

The core emotions of vulnerable partners with an emotional deprivation schema are loneliness, bitterness, disappointment, and depression. Their core behaviors are avoiding asking for their needs to be met and acting as if they do not have needs. Their worldview is that others will not meet their needs. The coping behaviors of people who have surrendered to this schema are to choose cold and detached partners.

These behaviors are contrasted by the overcompensating behavior of critical partners with an emotional deprivation schema, whom you read about in chapter 1. They demand that other people meet all of their needs and become critical when their needs go unmet.

♥ Michael's Story

Michael was the eldest of six children. His father was a colonel in the army, requiring the family to move seven times between Michael's birth and high-school graduation. Michael's mother was a sweet woman with a quiet disposition, which seemed like an accomplishment, given that her life involved moving every couple of years while giving birth to six children in a nine-year span.

A very disciplined man, Michael's father imposed the same discipline on his children. When he came home from work, the children were not to disturb him, a routine that remained the same for as long as Michael could remember. His father came home from work, removed his military uniform, and replaced it with khakis and a crisp, white button-down shirt. His father would go to the living room, where he and Michael's mother would exchange conversation over his drink of choice, scotch on the rocks with three ice cubes. During this time the children were expected to entertain themselves quietly. As the eldest, Michael was expected to enforce this rule with his siblings.

When the children were called for dinner at exactly 6:30 p.m., they were expected to sit quietly, use their table manners when eating and drinking, and speak only when their father addressed them. Michael's father always addressed the youngest child first. He asked all the children, one at a time, a question about their day, and each child responded appropriately. There were rarely any private exchanges between the children and their parents.

Michael was never given the opportunity to express his needs. The only physical affection that he received was a good morning salute and a nightly pat on the back from his father, and a good-night kiss on his forehead from his mother. There was never an opportunity for an exchange of ideas or feelings. Michael came to believe that others would never meet his needs. Michael's childhood history makes him vulnerable to behavior and situations that trigger his emotional deprivation schema.

Michael left home for college and entered a world that was completely foreign to him. His friendships in his childhood and adolescent years had been confined to schoolmates. Michael didn't date in high school. Girls seemed to be attracted to him, but with his family's schedule, there hadn't been any time for him to explore the possibility of a relationship.

When Michael moved into his coed dorm, he was fascinated by the mix of people and the free-flowing nature of his new environment. His roommate, Jeff, seemed like a good guy. Outgoing and very comfortable interacting with girls, Jeff always included Michael when he headed to the common room to socialize, or to the cafeteria to eat and socialize. Everyone liked Michael. He was good-looking, easygoing, and a great listener. The girls loved talking to him because he really seemed to care about them and their problems. Michael enjoyed having a more intimate connection with people, after being raised in a household where such connections didn't exist.

Because of Michael's lack of experience with sharing his feelings, he had a difficult time letting a girl named Becky know that he was interested in her beyond the friendship that they had developed. But without any discussion, their friendship suddenly turned into more than platonic when they spent the night together in her dorm room after a party. Always excited to see Michael, Becky called him regularly to hang out, but he soon recognized that the pattern of interaction between them was always the same: they got together when Becky wanted to get together, and they talked about what she wanted to talk about. When Michael called her to hang out, she didn't respond to him the way that he responded to her. Sometimes she could even come across as dismissive if he called her at an inconvenient time. Michael didn't know how to talk to her about what he was feeling. He didn't want to say anything to Becky that might annoy her. He was still stinging from her response to him the night he called to ask her if he could come over and spend the night with her: "Michael, I really can't handle it if you are going to be needy. I have too much going on to handle your demands." Michael figured out that it was better for his relationship with Becky if he didn't express his needs.

Vulnerable Partner Schema: Abandonment

The core emotions of vulnerable partners with an abandonment schema are anxiety, sadness, depression, and anger. Their core behavior is to cling to their partners, and their worldview is the belief that people close to them will leave them, get sick and die, or behave unpredictably. The coping behavior of people who are surrendering to this schema is to choose partners who are unpredictable or unavailable. This typical partner choice seems counterintuitive for people with this type of life experience, but they are drawn to what they know and are giving in to their schema.

This behavior differs from the coping behavior of critical partners with an abandonment schema, who overcompensate for their schema by attacking, withdrawing, possessing, and controlling their partners.

♥ Kevin's Story

The youngest of four children who grew up on a working farm in Wyoming, Kevin was nicknamed the "big surprise" because his parents already had a fourteen-year-old daughter and eighteen-year-old twin sons when his mother realized that she was pregnant with Kevin. As a little kid, Kevin remembers following his mom around the house as she did her chores in the morning and then being her little helper in the afternoon when she tended to their family garden. His older siblings had bigger responsibilities, like feeding the chickens and livestock and driving the tractors. Kevin's dad was out in the fields from sunup to sundown, six days a week. But when he was home, he was always fun. His dad was a happy man who loved to play with his children. He was a big, strong man, who took great pride in providing for his family. And his family was filled with love and affection.

His dad's death of a massive heart attack when Kevin was twelve years old left a huge hole in their family. It was an enormous loss for Kevin, his mom, and his siblings. Kevin's mom suffered deeply after her husband's death. She was constantly fatigued, had persistent abdominal pain, and was losing weight at a steady rate, symptoms that were attributed to her grief until she visited her gynecologist for her annual checkup. After running some tests, the doctor told her that she had ovarian cancer and only had a couple of months left to live. Kevin's mom died two months after her diagnosis.

After his parents' deaths, Kevin became very anxious about being alone, so his siblings, who still lived at home and worked the family farm, each took a turn at sharing a bedroom with him. Kevin found it difficult to be away from any of his siblings. Getting him to school every day was a challenge. He always worried about what he might find when he got home. Once he was home and reassured that his siblings were fine, his anxiety would subside. Kevin believed that the people close to him would leave him. Kevin's childhood history makes him vulnerable to behaviors and situations that trigger his abandonment schema.

When Kevin finished high school, he and his siblings decided that it would be best for him to continue to live at home with them. He would get a job in Cheyenne, a city an hour away from their farm. They wanted Kevin to gain some independence and develop relationships outside of his immediate family while still having the security of his home life.

Kevin got a job working at a diner in Cheyenne. He worked the day shift as a dishwasher. An energetic, fun, and engaging guy, Kevin quickly made friends at work and developed a crush on the owner's daughter, Katie. While taking classes at the local junior college, Katie came into the diner several times a day, whenever she had longer breaks between classes. It was obvious to everyone that the feelings between Kevin and Katie were mutual. They started hanging out several evenings a week after Kevin finished work. Kevin would have spent every evening with her, but she seemed to like to keep things more casual.

Kevin thought that things were going well between the two of them but then started to worry that something was wrong. Katie stopped coming to the diner every day. The first time it happened, Kevin called her in a panic to make sure that she was okay. She quickly reassured him that she was fine, but didn't stay on the phone to talk. Kevin tried to be cool about it, but when she didn't meet him at the diner for one of their usual evenings out together, he called her and begged her to let him come over because he really needed to see her. She agreed that he could come over for fifteen minutes, but when he arrived, Katie was very distant toward him. When Kevin asked her if something was wrong, she told him that she was just tired and needed to get some sleep. Kevin went home but stayed up all night worrying that Katie was going to leave him. The next day, Katie showed up at the diner and behaved as if everything were fine. Kevin felt better, but Katie's unpredictability and unreliability triggered his abandonment schema.

Summary

This chapter presented the five primary schemas associated with vulnerable partners and their corresponding core emotions, core behaviors, worldviews, and partner selection. The stories in this chapter are not designed to represent the only childhood experiences that could contribute to the formation of an early maladaptive schema, but to highlight a sampling of experiences that could leave people vulnerable to situations and behaviors that trigger their early maladaptive schemas. The stories about how each early maladaptive schema influenced each person in adulthood are not the only possible outcomes; they are simply meant to represent the enduring pattern of the schemas. The following chapter will provide the necessary tools for you to identify your early maladaptive schema, as well its origin.

Vulnerable Partner Schemas

Subjugation

- *Core emotions:* Fear, anxiety, and depression.
- *Core behaviors:* Takes care of other people before herself and allows herself to be controlled by partner.
- *Worldview:* Needs and wants of others come before his own needs and wants, he matters less than others do, and it is bad for him to have his own needs and desires.
- *Partner selection:* Drawn to dominant, controlling partners with whom she is compliant.

Defectiveness

- *Core emotions:* Shame and fear.
- *Core behaviors:* Self-conscious and compares himself to others.
- *Worldview:* She is defective, bad, unwanted, inferior, or invalid.
- *Partner selection:* Chooses critical partners.

Mistrust and Abuse

- *Core emotions:* Fear and anxiety.
- *Core behaviors:* Guarded and suspicious.
- *Worldview:* People cannot be trusted.
- *Partner selection:* Chooses unpredictable and untrustworthy partners.

Emotional Deprivation

- *Core emotions:* Loneliness, bitterness, disappointment, and depression.
- *Core behaviors:* Not asking for his needs to be met and acting as if he does not have needs.
- *Worldview:* Others will not meet her needs.
- *Partner selection:* Chooses cold and detached partners.

Abandonment

- *Core emotions:* Anxiety, sadness, depression, and anger.
- *Core behavior:* Clings to his partners.
- *Worldview:* People close to her will leave her, get sick and die, or behave unpredictably.
- *Partner selection:* Chooses partners who are unpredictable or unavailable.

Chapter 4

Uncovering Your Schema

Now it is time for you to think about your own childhood and adolescent years. Because you will be focusing on your own experiences, you may find this process easier than the one for your partner. However, because you have a greater emotional connection to your experiences, this process might be challenging for you. To provide clarity, you will use the same procedure for recording your childhood history that you did for your partner in chapter 2. You may have already identified your schema from the descriptions and stories in the previous chapter. If so, after you complete your childhood history form, skip to the worksheet for the schema that you have identified as yours. If you are uncertain about which schema resonates with you or if you feel that more than one schema could be a match for you, then fill out all of the worksheets. As you fill them out, if you find yourself torn about what rating to give a statement in the worksheet, go with the response that comes from your emotional reaction. Try to stay in your childhood and adolescent experience when you rate the statements.

Your Childhood History

Mother:

_____

_____

_____

_____

_____

Father:

_____

_____

_____

_____

_____

Siblings:

_____

_____

_____

_____

_____

Peers:

_____

_____

_____

_____

_____

Experiences:

_____

_____

_____

_____

_____

_____

Vulnerable Partner Schema: Subjugation

Susan filled out the following childhood history worksheet. Later you'll find two blank worksheets for you to fill out, along with sample worksheets that Susan completed as part of her assessment.

Susan's Childhood History

Mother:

Perfect wife.

Always agreed with her husband.

Accommodating to her three sons.

Treated me as if I didn't matter as much as the men in the family.

Father:

Chief of surgery.

Decision maker.

Controlling.

Male chauvinist.

Siblings:

Three older brothers.

Everything was always about them.

Peers:

Had lots of friends.

Let my friends determine what we did.

Experiences:

Parents made me play tennis even though I preferred swimming. My feelings and opinions mattered less than theirs.

Worksheet 4.1: Is Your Early Maladaptive Schema Subjugation?

Adapted from the Young Schema Questionnaire with the permission and assistance of Jeffrey Young, Ph.D., the following statements are designed to help you identify your early maladaptive schema. Try to rate the statements from an honest and undefended place.

Rating Scale

1 = completely untrue

2 = mostly untrue

3 = slightly more true than untrue

4 = moderately true

5 = mostly true

6 = absolutely true

Statement	Rating
1. I let other people control me and my life.	
2. I worry that if I don't fulfill the wishes of others, they will get angry and retaliate or reject me.	
3. The major decisions in my life have not been in my control.	
4. I have difficulty demanding that other people respect my rights.	
5. I really worry about pleasing people and getting their approval.	
6. I go to great lengths to avoid conflict or confrontations with others.	
7. I give more to others than they give to me.	
8. I experience other people's pain deeply, which leads me to take care of the people I'm close to.	
9. If I put myself first, I feel guilty.	
10. I am a good person because I think of others more than I think of myself.	
Total: _____	

Interpreting Your Ratings

10–19   Very low. This schema probably does not apply to you.

20–29   Fairly low. This schema may only apply occasionally.

30–39 Moderate. This schema is an issue in your life.

40–49 High. This is definitely an important schema for you.

50–60 Very high. This is definitely one of your core schemas.

If you rated any of the statements as 5 or 6, this schema may still apply to you, even if the total is in the low range.

Susan filled out the following worksheet to determine her early maladaptive schema.

Sample Worksheet 4.1: Susan's Ratings on Whether Her Early Maladaptive Schema Is Subjugation

Statement	Rating
1. I let other people control me and my life.	5
2. I worry that if I don't fulfill the wishes of others, they will get angry and retaliate or reject me.	5
3. The major decisions in my life have not been in my control.	5
4. I have difficulty demanding that other people respect my rights.	5
5. I really worry about pleasing people and getting their approval.	4
6. I go to great lengths to avoid conflict or confrontations with others.	5
7. I give more to others than they give to me.	4

8. I experience other people's pain deeply, which leads me to take care of the people I'm close to.	3
9. If I put myself first, I feel guilty.	4
10. I am a good person because I think of others more than I think of myself.	3
Total:	43

Susan gave five statements a rating of 5. Based on these ratings and a total of 43, Susan determined that she has a subjugation schema.

Worksheet 4.2 Uncover the Origin of Your Subjugation Schema

Adapted from the Young Schema Questionnaire with the permission and assistance of Jeffrey Young, Ph.D., the following statements will help you identify the origins of your early maladaptive schema. Think about your mother and father, or primary caregiver in the absence of your mother and father. Rate the following statements as accurately as possible based on your childhood experience.

Rating Scale

    1 = completely untrue

    2 = mostly untrue

    3 = slightly more true than untrue

    4 = moderately true

    5 = mostly true

    6 = absolutely true

The Critical Partner

Statement	Mother	Father
1. My mother/father tried to dominate or control major aspects of my life.		
2. My mother/father got angry at me and threatened or punished me when I wouldn't do things her/his way.		
3. My mother/father withdrew emotionally or cut off contact with me if I disagreed with her/him about how to do things.		
4. My mother/father did not allow me to make my own choices as a child.		
5. My mother/father was not around much or was incapable, so I ended up taking care of the rest of the family.		
6. My mother/father always talked to me about her/his personal problems, so I was always in the role of listener.		
7. My mother/father made me feel guilty or selfish if I didn't do what she/he wanted.		
8. My mother/father was like a martyr or saint: she/he selflessly took care of everyone else and denied her/his own needs.		
9. My mother/father did not respect my rights, needs, or opinions when I was a child.		
10. I had to be careful about what I said or did as a child because I was concerned that my mother/father would become worried or depressed.		

11. As a child, I felt angry at my mother/father for not giving me the freedom that other children had.		

Ratings: If you noted 4, 5, or 6 for any of the statements, add up how many times you wrote each of these ratings for your mother and father.

	4	5	6
Mother			
Father			

Interpreting Your Ratings

Count the number of times you marked 4, 5, or 6 to describe your mother or father. If you noted one or more of these ratings, you have likely identified the origin of your early maladaptive schema.

Susan filled out the following worksheet to determine the origin of her early maladaptive schema.

Sample Worksheet 4.2: Susan's Ratings on the Origin of Her Subjugation Schema

Statement	Mother	Father
1. My mother/father tried to dominate or control major aspects of my life.	5	5
2. My mother/father got angry at me and threatened or punished me when I wouldn't do things her/his way.	2	2
3. My mother/father withdrew emotionally or cut off contact with me if I disagreed with her/him about how to do things.	2	2

4. My mother/father did not allow me to make my own choices as a child.	6	6
5. My mother/father was not around much or was incapable, so I ended up taking care of the rest of the family.	1	1
6. My mother/father always talked to me about her/his personal problems, so I was always in the role of listener.	1	1
7. My mother/father made me feel guilty or selfish if I didn't do what she/he wanted.	2	2
8. My mother/father was like a martyr or saint: she/he selflessly took care of everyone else and denied her/his own needs.	4	1
9. My mother/father did not respect my rights, needs, or opinions when I was a child.	5	5
10. I had to be careful about what I said or did as a child because I was concerned that my mother/father would become worried or depressed.	1	1
11. As a child, I felt angry at my mother/father for not giving me the freedom that other children had.	2	2

Ratings: If you noted 4, 5, or 6 for any of the statements, add up how many times you wrote each of these ratings for your mother and father.

	4	5	6
Mother	1	2	1
Father	0	2	1

Susan marked 4 once for her mother, and 5 twice and 6 once for each of her parents. Both of Susan's parents are the origin of her subjugation schema.

Vulnerable Partner Schema: Defectiveness and Shame

Rachel filled out the following childhood history worksheet. Later you'll find two blank worksheets, along with two sample worksheets that Rachel completed as part of her assessment.

Rachel's Childhood History

Mother:

Couldn't cope with me.

Didn't enjoy me.

Believed that I was a problem.

Father:

Was an unhappy father with me.

Rejected me in favor of my sister.

Siblings:

Younger sister was perfect.

Peers:

Was attracted to friends and boyfriends who weren't particularly nice to me and often made critical comments.

Experiences:

<u>*My parents left me alone to console myself.*</u>

<u>*My parents constantly compared me to my perfect sister.*</u>

Worksheet 4.3: Is Your Early Maladaptive Schema Defectiveness and Shame?

Adapted from the Young Schema Questionnaire with the permission and assistance of Jeffrey Young, Ph.D., the following statements are designed to help you identify your early maladaptive schema. Try to rate the statements from an honest and undefended place.

Rating Scale

1 = completely untrue

2 = mostly untrue

3 = slightly more true than untrue

4 = moderately true

5 = mostly true

6 = absolutely true

Statement	Rating
1. Someone who really knew me couldn't love me.	
2. Because I am inherently flawed and defective, I am not worthy of love.	
3. I have secrets that I will not share, even with the people closest to me.	

4. I am to blame for my parents' inability to love me.	
5. I present a false self that hides the real me because the real me is unacceptable.	
6. I tend to be drawn to people who are critical and rejecting of me.	
7. I tend to be critical and rejecting of others, especially those who seem to love me.	
8. I tend to devalue my positive qualities.	
9. I feel a lot of shame about myself.	
10. Exposure of my faults is one of my greatest fears.	
Total: _____	

Interpreting Your Ratings

10–19   Very low. This schema probably does not apply to you.

20–29   Fairly low. This schema may only apply occasionally.

30–39   Moderate. This schema is an issue in your life.

40–49   High. This is definitely an important schema for you.

50–60   Very high. This is definitely one of your core schemas.

If you rated any of the statements as 5 or 6, this schema may still apply to you, even if the total is in the low range.

Rachel filled out the following worksheet to determine her early maladaptive schema.

Sample Worksheet 4.3: Rachel's Ratings on Whether Her Early Maladaptive Schema Is Defectiveness and Shame

Statement	Rating
1. Someone who really knew me couldn't love me.	5
2. Because I am inherently flawed and defective, I am not worthy of love.	5
3. I have secrets that I will not share, even with the people closest to me.	4
4. I am to blame for my parents' inability to love me.	5
5. I present a false self that hides the real me because the real me is unacceptable.	4
6. I tend to be drawn to people who are critical and rejecting of me.	6
7. I tend to be critical and rejecting of others, especially those who seem to love me.	2
8. I tend to devalue my positive qualities.	5
9. I feel a lot of shame about myself.	4
10. Exposure of my faults is one of my greatest fears.	4
Total:	44

Rachel gave four statements a rating of 5 and one statement a rating of 6. Based on these ratings and a total of 44, Rachel determined that she has a defectiveness and shame schema.

Worksheet 4.4: Uncover the Origin of Your Defectiveness and Shame Schema

Adapted from the Young Schema Questionnaire with the permission and assistance of Jeffrey Young, Ph.D., the following statements will help you identify the origin of your early maladaptive schema. Think about your mother and father, or your primary caregiver in the absence of your mother and father. Rate the following statements as accurately as possible based on your childhood experience.

Rating Scale

1 = completely untrue

2 = mostly untrue

3 = slightly more true than untrue

4 = moderately true

5 = mostly true

6 = absolutely true

Statement	Mother	Father
1. My mother/father was extremely critical, demeaning, or punitive toward me.		
2. My mother/father repeatedly criticized or punished me for my appearance, behavior, or things I said.		
3. My mother/father rejected me or made me feel unloved as a child.		
4. My mother/father abused me sexually, physically, or emotionally when I was a child.		

5. My mother/father regularly blamed me when things went wrong in our family.		
6. My mother/father told me repeatedly that I was bad, worthless, or good-for-nothing.		
7. My mother/father repeatedly compared me in an unfavorable way to my sibling(s).		
8. My mother/father left home when I was a child, and I blamed myself.		
9. My mother/father made me feel ashamed of myself or her/him.		

Ratings: If you noted 4, 5, or 6 for any of the statements, add up how many times you wrote each of these ratings for your mother and father.

	4	5	6
Mother			
Father			

Interpreting Your Ratings

Count the number of times you marked 4, 5, or 6 to describe your mother or father. If you noted one or more of these ratings, you have likely identified the origin of your early maladaptive schema.

———————————————————————————

Rachel filled out the following worksheet to determine the origin of her early maladaptive schema.

Sample Worksheet 4.4: Rachel's Ratings on the Origin of Her Defectiveness and Shame Schema

Statement	Mother	Father
1. My mother/father was extremely critical, demeaning, or punitive toward me.	4	4
2. My mother/father repeatedly criticized or punished me for my appearance, behavior, or things I said.	5	5
3. My mother/father rejected me or made me feel unloved as a child.	5	5
4. My mother/father abused me sexually, physically, or emotionally when I was a child.	2	2
5. My mother/father regularly blamed me when things went wrong in our family.	5	5
6. My mother/father told me repeatedly that I was bad, worthless, or good-for-nothing.	4	4
7. My mother/father repeatedly compared me in an unfavorable way to my sibling(s).	6	6
8. My mother/father left home when I was a child, and I blamed myself.	1	1
9. My mother/father made me feel ashamed of myself or her/him.	4	4

	4	5	6
Mother	3	3	1
Father	3	3	1

Ratings: If you noted 4, 5, or 6 for any of the statements, add up how many times you wrote each of these ratings for your mother and father.

Rachel marked three ratings of 4, three ratings of 5, and one rating of 6 for each of her parents. She determined that both of her parents are the origin of her defectiveness and shame schema.

Vulnerable Partner Schema: Mistrust and Abuse

The following is the childhood history form that Julie filled out. Later you'll find two worksheets that she completed as part of her assessment.

Julie's Childhood History

Mother:

Kept the secret from me and my twin brother that our father was not our biological father and that the family friend we called Uncle James was our biological father.

Father:

Left our family home when the truth came out that he was not our biological father.

Siblings:

Twin brother, John—close to him; leaned on each other a lot.

Peers:

Prior to my mother's betrayal, I had lots of friends.

When I was shipped off to boarding school, I didn't keep in touch with people and was slow
to make new friends.

Experiences:

Walked in on my mother and Uncle James in my parents' bedroom.

Worksheet 4.5: Is Your Early Maladaptive Schema Mistrust and Abuse?

Adapted from the Young Schema Questionnaire with the permission and assistance of Jeffrey Young, Ph.D., the following statements are designed to help you identify your early maladaptive schema. Try to rate the statements from an honest and undefended place.

Rating Scale

1 = completely untrue

2 = mostly untrue

3 = slightly more true than untrue

4 = moderately true

5 = mostly true

6 = absolutely true

Statement	Rating
1. I have the expectation that people will hurt me or use me.	
2. People close to me have consistently abused me.	
3. I know that it is only a matter of time before the people who are important in my life betray me.	

4. I must protect myself and be on guard.	
5. People will take advantage of me if I am not careful.	
6. I regularly set up tests for people to determine if they are really on my side.	
7. I tend to hurt others before they can hurt me.	
8. I fear that people will hurt me if I allow them to get close to me.	
9. When I think about what people have done to me, I get angry.	
10. The people whom I should have been able to trust have physically, verbally, or sexually abused me.	
Total: _____	

Interpreting Your Ratings

10–19   Very low. This schema probably does not apply to you.

20–29   Fairly low. This schema may only apply occasionally.

30–39   Moderate. This schema is an issue in your life.

40–49   High. This is definitely an important schema for you.

50–60   Very high. This is definitely one of your core schemas.

If you rated any of the statements as 5 or 6, this schema may still apply to you, even if the total is in the low range.

Julie filled out the following worksheet to determine her early maladaptive schema.

Sample Worksheet 4.5: Julie's Ratings on Whether Her Early Maladaptive Schema Is Mistrust and Abuse

Statement	Rating
1. I have the expectation that people will hurt me or use me.	5
2. People close to me have consistently abused me.	2
3. I know that it is only a matter of time before the people who are important in my life betray me.	5
4. I must protect myself and be on guard.	5
5. People will take advantage of me if I am not careful.	2
6. I regularly set up tests for people to determine if they are really on my side.	4
7. I tend to hurt others before they can hurt me.	2
8. I fear that people will hurt me if I allow them to get close to me.	4
9. When I think about what people have done to me, I get angry.	2
10. The people whom I should have been able to trust have physically, verbally, or sexually abused me.	1
Total:	32

Julie gave three statements a rating of 5. Based on these ratings and a total of 32, Julie determined that she has a mistrust and abuse schema.

Worksheet 4.6: Uncover the Origin of Your Mistrust and Abuse Schema

Adapted from the Young Schema Questionnaire with the permission and assistance of Jeffrey Young, Ph.D., the following statements will help you identify the origin of your early maladaptive schema. Think about your mother and father, or your primary caregiver in the absence of your mother and father. Rate the following statements as accurately as possible based on your childhood experience.

Rating Scale

    1 = completely untrue

    2 = mostly untrue

    3 = slightly more true than untrue

    4 = moderately true

    5 = mostly true

    6 = absolutely true

Statement	Mother	Father
1. My mother/father physically abused me as a child.		
2. My mother/father sexually abused me or repeatedly touched me in a sexually provocative way when I was a child.		
3. My mother/father verbally or emotionally abused me, or both (for example, repeatedly humiliated me, teased me, or put me down).		

4. My mother/father seemed to take pleasure in seeing me suffer.			
5. My mother/father threatened me with severe punishment or retaliation to get me to do things.			
6. My mother/father regularly warned me not to trust people outside of our family.			
7. My mother/father made me feel that she/he was against me.			
8. My mother/father betrayed me in a way that made me feel that I couldn't trust her/him.			

Ratings: If you noted 4, 5, or 6 for any of the statements, add up how many times you wrote each of these ratings for your mother and father.

	4	5	6
Mother			
Father			

Interpreting Your Ratings

Count the number of times you marked 4, 5, or 6 to describe your mother or father. If you noted one or more of these ratings, you have likely identified the origin of your early maladaptive schema.

Julie filled out the following worksheet to determine the origin of her early maladaptive schema.

Sample Worksheet 4.6: Julie's Ratings on the Origin of Her Mistrust and Abuse Schema

Statement	Mother	Father
1. My mother/father physically abused me as a child.	1	1
2. My mother/father sexually abused me or repeatedly touched me in a sexually provocative way when I was a child.	1	1
3. My mother/father verbally or emotionally abused me, or both (for example, repeatedly humiliated me, teased me, or put me down).	1	1
4. My mother/father seemed to take pleasure in seeing me suffer.	1	1
5. My mother/father threatened me with severe punishment or retaliation to get me to do things.	1	1
6. My mother/father regularly warned me not to trust people outside of our family.	1	1
7. My mother/father made me feel that she/he was against me.	1	1
8. My mother/father betrayed me in a way that made me feel that I couldn't trust her/him.	6	1

Ratings: If you noted 4, 5, or 6 for any of the statements, add up how many times you wrote each of these ratings for your mother and father.			
	4	5	6
Mother	0	0	1
Father	0	0	0

Julie gave one statement about her mother a rating of 6. This is enough to determine that her mother is the origin of her early maladaptive schema.

Vulnerable Partner Schema: Emotional Deprivation

Michael filled out the following childhood history worksheet. Later you'll find two blank worksheets, plus two sample worksheets that Michael completed as part of his assessment.

Michael's Childhood History

Mother:

Had six children.

Sweet and quiet.

Not affectionate but kind.

Didn't talk about feelings or anything personal.

Father:

Colonel in the army.

Disciplined, routine, driven, and stoic.

Very brief interaction with each child.

Didn't express feelings or encourage the expression of feelings.

Siblings:

Two younger sisters.

Three younger brothers.

Siblings viewed me as another parental figure, so there was no fun interaction or emotional connectedness with them.

Peers:

Family life was too structured to have friends over or develop anything more than superficial friendships.

Experiences:

Father saluted me in the morning and patted me on the back at night.

Mother kissed me good night on my forehead.

When I was thirteen, my father gave me a book to read that explained "the birds and the bees," but we never discussed it.

Worksheet 4.7: Is Your Early Maladaptive Schema Emotional Deprivation?

Adapted from the Young Schema Questionnaire with the permission and assistance of Jeffrey Young, Ph.D., the following statements are designed to help you identify your early maladaptive schema. Try to rate the statements from an honest and undefended place.

Rating Scale

1 = completely untrue

2 = mostly untrue

3 = slightly more true than untrue

4 = moderately true

5 = mostly true

6 = absolutely true

Statement	Rating
1. I don't get as much love as I need.	
2. I feel as if no one really understands me.	
3. I am usually attracted to cold partners who can't meet my needs.	
4. I don't feel connected, even to the people who are closest to me.	
5. I have not had one special person in my life who wants to share himself/herself with me and cares about what happens to me.	
6. I don't have anyone in my life to hold me or give me warmth and affection.	
7. I do not have a person in my life who really listens and is tuned in to my true needs and feelings.	
8. I find it difficult to let people guide or protect me, even though it is what I want.	
9. I find it difficult to let people love me.	
10. I feel lonely most of the time.	
Total: _____	

Interpreting Your Ratings

10–19   Very low. This schema probably does not apply to you.

20–29   Fairly low. This schema may only apply occasionally.

30–39   Moderate. This schema is an issue in your life.

40–49   High. This is definitely an important schema for you.

50–60   Very high. This is definitely one of your core schemas.

If you rated any of the statements as 5 or 6, this schema may still apply to you, even if the total is in the low range.

Michael filled out the following worksheet to determine his early maladaptive schema.

Sample Worksheet 4.7: Michael's Ratings on Whether His Early Maladaptive Schema Is Emotional Deprivation

Statement	Rating
1. I don't get as much love as I need.	5
2. I feel as if no one really understands me.	5
3. I am usually attracted to cold partners who can't meet my needs.	5
4. I don't feel connected, even to the people who are closest to me.	3
5. I have not had one special person in my life who wants to share himself/herself with me and cares about what happens to me.	6

6. I don't have anyone in my life to hold me or give me warmth and affection.	6
7. I do not have a person in my life who really listens and is tuned in to my true needs and feelings.	5
8. I find it difficult to let people guide or protect me, even though it is what I want.	2
9. I find it difficult to let people love me.	2
10. I feel lonely most of the time.	5
Total:	__44__

Michael gave five statements a rating of 5 and two statements a rating of 6. Based on these ratings and a total of 44, Michael determined that he has an emotional deprivation schema.

Worksheet 4.8: Uncover the Origin of Your Emotional Deprivation Schema

Adapted from the Young Schema Questionnaire with the permission and assistance of Jeffrey Young, Ph.D., the following statements can help you identify the origins of your early maladaptive schema. Think about your mother and father, or your primary caregiver in the absence of your mother and father. Rate the following statements as accurately as possible based on your childhood experience.

Rating Scale

1 = completely untrue

2 = mostly untrue

3 = slightly more true than untrue

4 = moderately true

5 = mostly true

6 = absolutely true

Statement	Mother	Father
1. My mother/father was cold and unaffectionate with me when I was a child.		
2. My mother/father did not make me feel loved and valued. She/he did not make me feel special.		
3. My mother/father did not give me adequate time and attention.		
4. My mother/father was not tuned in to my needs when I was a child.		
5. My mother/father did not give me adequate guidance when I was a child.		
6. My mother/father was not solid enough for me to feel that I could rely on her/him.		
Ratings: If you noted 4, 5, or 6 for any of the statements, add up how many times you wrote each of these ratings for your mother and father.		

	4	5	6
Mother			
Father			

Interpreting Your Ratings

Count the number of times you marked 4, 5, or 6 for your mother and father. If you noted one or more of any of those numbers, it is likely that you have identified the origin of your early maladaptive schema.

Michael filled out the following worksheet to determine the origin of his early maladaptive schema.

Sample Worksheet 4.8: Michael's Ratings on the Origin of His Emotional Deprivation Schema

Statement	Mother	Father
1. My mother/father was cold and unaffectionate with me when I was a child.	4	4
2. My mother/father did not make me feel loved and valued. She/he did not make me feel special.	3	4
3. My mother/father did not give me adequate time and attention.	4	5
4. My mother/father was not tuned in to my needs when I was a child.	3	3
5. My mother/father did not give me adequate guidance when I was a child.	2	2
6. My mother/father was not solid enough for me to feel that I could rely on her/him.	1	1

Ratings: If you noted 4, 5, or 6 for any of the statements, add up how many times you wrote each of these ratings for your mother and father.

	4	5	6
Mother	2	0	0
Father	2	1	0

Michael gave his mother two ratings of 4 and his father two ratings of 4 and one rating of 5. Both of Michael's parents are the origin of his early maladaptive schema.

Vulnerable Partner Schema: Abandonment

Kevin filled out the following childhood history worksheet. Later you'll find two blank worksheets, plus two sample worksheets that Kevin completed as part of his assessment.

Kevin's Childhood History

Mother:

Loving.

Caring.

Affectionate.

Father:

Happy.

Fun.

Hardworking.

Loving.

Siblings:

Sister, fourteen years older.

Twin brothers, eighteen years older.

Very close—loving and affectionate.

Peers:

Close-knit family living on a farm in a sparsely populated area, not conducive to developing friendships outside of school.

Had friendships at school.

Experiences:

Dad died of a massive heart attack when I was twelve years old.

Mom died two months after being diagnosed with ovarian cancer.

Worksheet 4.9: Is Your Early Maladaptive Schema Abandonment?

Adapted from the Young Schema Questionnaire with the permission and assistance of Jeffrey Young, Ph.D., the following statements are designed to help you identify your early maladaptive schema. Try to rate the statements from an honest and undefended place.

Rating Scale

1 = completely untrue

2 = mostly untrue

3 = slightly more true than untrue

4 = moderately true

5 = mostly true

6 = absolutely true

Statement	Rating
1. I am fearful that people I love will die or leave me.	
2. I get clingy with people when I feel that they are going to leave me.	
3. My support system feels unstable	
4. I find myself falling in love with people who aren't capable of committing to me or willing to do so.	

5. People have always moved in and out of my life.	
6. When someone I love pulls away, I feel desperate.	
7. My obsession with the idea that my lovers will leave me drives them away.	
8. The people with whom I have the closest relationships are unpredictable. Sometimes they are there for me, and sometimes they are not.	
9. I feel as if I need people more than others do.	
10. I feel as if I will be alone toward the end of my life.	
Total: _____	

Interpreting Your Ratings

10–19   Very low. This schema probably does not apply to you.

20–29   Fairly low. This schema may only apply occasionally.

30–39   Moderate. This schema is an issue in your life.

40–49   High. This is definitely an important schema for you.

50–60   Very high. This is definitely one of your core schemas.

If you rated any of the statements as 5 or 6, this schema may still apply to you, even if the total is in the low range.

Kevin filled out the following worksheet to determine his early maladaptive schema.

Sample Worksheet 4.9: Kevin's Ratings on Whether His Early Maladaptive Schema Is Abandonment

Statement	Rating
1. I am fearful that people I love will die or leave me.	6
2. I get clingy with people when I feel that they are going to leave me.	5
3. My support system feels unstable.	1
4. I find myself falling in love with people who aren't capable of committing to me or willing to do so.	5
5. People have always moved in and out of my life.	1
6. When someone I love pulls away, I feel desperate.	5
7. My obsession with the idea that my lovers will leave me drives them away.	3
8. The people with whom I have the closest relationships are unpredictable. Sometimes they are there for me, and sometimes they are not.	1
9. I feel as if I need people more than others do.	4
10. I feel as if I will be alone toward the end of my life.	4
Total:	_35_

Kevin gave three statements a rating of 5 and one statement a rating of 6. Based on these ratings and a total of 35, Kevin determined that he has an abandonment schema.

Worksheet 4.10: Uncover the Origin of Your Abandonment Schema

Adapted from the Young Schema Questionnaire with the permission and assistance of Jeffrey Young, Ph.D., the following statements will help you identify the origins of your early maladaptive schema. Think about your mother and father, or your primary caregiver in the absence of your mother and father. Rate the following statements as accurately as possible based on your childhood experience.

Rating Scale

1 = completely untrue

2 = mostly untrue

3 = slightly more true than untrue

4 = moderately true

5 = mostly true

6 = absolutely true

Statement	Mother	Father
1. My mother/father died or left home when I was young.		
2. My mother/father preferred my sibling(s) to me.		
3. My mother/father was unstable.		
4. My mother/father suffered from depression and withdrew from me on a regular basis.		
5. My mother/father was unpredictable and withdrew from me on a regular basis.		

6. My mother/father was addicted to drugs, alcohol, or both, and would "check out" frequently.		

Ratings: If you noted 4, 5, or 6 for any of the statements, add up how many times you wrote each of these ratings for your mother and father.

	4	5	6
Mother			
Father			

Interpreting Your Ratings

Count the number of times you marked 4, 5, or 6 to describe your mother or father. If you noted one or more of these ratings, you have likely identified the origin of your early maladaptive schema.

Kevin filled out the following worksheet to determine the origin of his early maladaptive schema.

Sample Worksheet 4.10: Kevin's Ratings on the Origin of His Abandonment Schema

Statement	Mother	Father
1. My mother/father died or left home when I was young.	6	6
2. My mother/father preferred my sibling(s) to me.	1	1
3. My mother/father was unstable.	1	1

4. My mother/father suffered from depression and withdrew from me on a regular basis.	1	1
5. My mother/father was unpredictable and withdrew from me on a regular basis.	1	1
6. My mother/father was addicted to drugs, alcohol, or both, and would "check out" frequently.	1	1

Ratings: If you noted 4, 5, or 6 for any of the statements, add up how many times you wrote each of these ratings for your mother and father.

	4	5	6
Mother	0	0	1
Father	0	0	1

Kevin gave each of his parents one rating of 6. This is enough to determine that both of Kevin's parents are the origin of his early maladaptive schema.

Summary

You have completed the final step in the assessment process. By this point you should have been able to identify both your partner's and your early maladaptive schemas. Your findings may surprise you. Maybe you and your partner have the same schema. You might be wondering how it is possible that two people could share such similar childhood experiences and have such a similar worldview, yet behave in such different ways. Or you may have discovered that you and your partner have different schemas, but through the examination process, you realized that your partner and one of your parents have similar behaviors. The next chapter will examine how schemas drive partner selection, the importance of coping behaviors, and the role of schema maintenance.

Chapter 5

Life Traps

Schemas are our identity. They form who we are, how we view our environment, how we interpret our interactions with others, and how we feel about ourselves. The largely unconscious behavioral strategies that we use in response to the activation of our schemas are meant to minimize the emotional pain associated with our schemas. These coping behaviors come from our attempts, beginning in childhood, to understand, control, or avoid painful events, thoughts, and feelings. Unfortunately, the three primary self-defeating coping behaviors people use in reaction to the high emotions that result from a schema-triggering experience are unhealthy responses to the schema that do not help to minimize the schema. In fact, they serve to reinforce it.

The purpose in identifying your dysfunctional schema-driven behavior and bringing it to awareness is to help you take the next step toward practicing healthy behaviors in response to the activation of your schema.

Three Primary Coping Behaviors

Jeffrey Young (2004) identified three maladaptive coping styles that people use to deal with their schemas: surrender, avoidance, and overcompensation.

Our schemas drive the three self-defeating behavior patterns that we use to cope with our schemas. Most people have one dominant coping behavior; however, it is common to unconsciously switch schema behaviors when dealing with different situations, people, or both.

Schema Surrender Behavior

Schema surrender behavior is acceptance of the schema. A person experiences the emotional pain of his schema, and his behavior serves as confirmation of that schema. Remember Susan, who was raised by parents who made all of her decisions for her without taking her preferences into consideration? She was made to feel that her opinion mattered less than the opinions of others, so she grew up feeling that her needs mattered less than the needs of others. She felt that she needed to take care of others before she took care of herself.

By choosing Kirk as a partner, Susan was surrendering to her subjugation schema. Kirk possesses many similar qualities to Susan's father. They are both doctors who expect their partners to accommodate their needs and demands before their own. If Susan continues to surrender to her schema, she will remain a prisoner of that schema.

Schema Avoidance Behavior

Schema avoidance behavior is a largely unconscious denial that the schema exists. On the surface this can appear to be a healthy behavioral response to an early maladaptive schema. However, if we look more closely, we can see that the person is withdrawing from important aspects that make for a full and happy life. Remember Michael's story? As the eldest of six children, he grew up with a strict and emotionally cold father and an overwhelmed mother. Michael's emotional needs were never met, and as an adult he concluded, based on his childhood experience, that his needs would never be met. We know from his adult relationship story that he was surrendering to his emotional deprivation schema, but let's see how things would look if Michael engaged in schema avoidance behavior. He would avoid intimate relationships as a way to eliminate the inevitable pain associated with the activation of his emotional deprivation schema. In avoiding intimate relationships, Michael would organize his life so that his schema would not get activated. If he withdrew from those relationships altogether, he would not risk experiencing the pain of having his emotional needs go unmet by a partner. This is a short-term solution for avoiding the pain associated with his schema, but it would not help to heal his schema.

Schema Overcompensation Behavior

Schema overcompensation, or counterattack, behavior is a battle against the schema. When a person is engaged in counterattack behavior as a reaction to her schema, she is combating the schema by behaving and relating to others as if the opposite of the schema were her experience.

Remember Beth and Joe's story from chapter 1? Joe's parents divorced when he was young, and as a teenager he was kicked out of the home that he shared with his mom and younger sister (the favorite child). Joe's counterattack behavior driven by his defectiveness and shame schema was to be critical of others, pointing out their flaws and defects. The instinct to fight against something that is harmful to you (in this case, an early maladaptive schema) is a natural and potentially good response. However, this behavior is unhealthy and emotionally destructive because it harms other people, especially loved ones. Joe's behavior toward Beth and her loved ones threatens their relationship, and if Joe's critical behavior continues, it will result in Beth's ending their relationship, which will ultimately reinforce the defectiveness schema that Joe is combating.

Beth told Joe that she loves him but can't continue to tolerate his behavior and the damage it is doing to their relationships with one another and with her family and friends. Beth encouraged Joe to examine his behavior by using the exercise for identifying schema-driven behavior. The following is how he completed the exercise. He has a defectiveness and shame schema, and when it is triggered, his coping behavior is overcompensation.

Use the blank worksheet that follows Joe's completed worksheet to identify and explore an event that triggered your schema.

Sample Exercise 5.1: Joe's Responses on Identifying Schema-Driven Behavior

Schema: _Defectiveness._

Event: _Beth and I went to dinner with two of Beth's childhood friends. They talked extensively about their successful new venture in the technology industry._

Thoughts: _I will never be as successful as Beth and her friends. I will never be successful enough to be good enough for Beth._

Action: _I asked questions and made statements that were critical of their new venture._

Reaction: _I upset Beth and alienated her friends._

Outcome: _It made me feel "less than" and as if something were wrong with me._

By identifying his schema-driven behavior, Joe is able to bring awareness to his self-defeating behaviors. Chapters 6 and 7 will present healthy alternative coping strategies that are designed to end the cycle of self-defeating behavior and the pain associated with it.

Exercise 5.1: Identify Schema-Driven Behavior

Schema: _____

Event: _____

_____

_____

_____

Thoughts: _____

_____

_____

_____

Action: _____

_____

_____

_____

Reaction: _____

_____

_____

_____

Outcome: _____

_____

_____

_____

What Determines Coping Behaviors

If you have already completed the schema assessment worksheets for yourself and your partner, you may have discovered that you and your partner have the same schema but your coping behaviors are different. Temperament plays a large role in what determines a person's schema-driven behavior. A person who is more aggressive will probably employ the overcompensation behavior, whereas a person who is more passive will more likely use surrender or avoidance behaviors. If we look at the four schemas that you and your critical partner could likely share and compare the overcompensating and surrendering coping behaviors, we will see how two people with the same schema can look so different. If your critical partner has the defectiveness and shame schema, he more than likely criticizes and rejects others while appearing to be perfect. If you have the defectiveness and shame schema, you probably put yourself down and choose critical or rejecting partners. If your critical partner has the mistrust and abuse schema, she likely uses and abuses others. If you have the mistrust and abuse schema, you likely select abusive partners and permit some degree of abuse. If your critical partner has the abandonment schema, he is probably jealous, possessive, and controlling. If you have the abandonment schema, you probably select partners who have a difficult time making a commitment. If your critical partner has an emotional deprivation schema, she likely demands that all of her needs be met. If you have the emotional deprivation schema, you likely do not ask for your needs to be met and select partners who are emotionally withholding. The four overlapping schemas with examples of overcompensating and surrendering coping behaviors show how temperament plays a major role in influencing behavior and how the coping behavior can make two people with the same schema look different.

Schema Magnets

Has anyone ever said, "He is totally your type," or "She is not the type of woman you are usually attracted to"? Other people say, "I don't have a type." According to Jeffrey Young (2004), each of us more than likely has a type that triggers an intense magnetic pull or chemistry. We probably don't realize that it is the result of the activation of an early maladaptive schema. Our schemas will be highly activated by a type of person who feels very familiar to us. We are all more comfortable when we are in the presence of someone or something familiar—even if the person or thing is not good for us. Consciously or unconsciously, we know what to expect and how to behave when we are interacting with someone or are in surroundings that feel familiar to us. There is always increased emotional arousal when a core schema is triggered.

What would make us consciously or unconsciously choose a partner who activates our schemas? First, *emotional arousal*—when a schema is triggered, there is a high emotional escalation; second, *cognitive consistency*—you are drawn to someone who reminds you of your family of origin; and third, *psychological drive*—your desire for a different outcome from your childhood experience (Young 2004).

Let's explore the idea of cognitive consistency and see if you can make a connection between one of your parents and your partner. Use the following exercise to list as many identifying characteristics and behaviors as possible for your mother, your father, and your partner.

Exercise 5.2: Cognitive Consistency

Mother: _____

Characteristics: _____

_____

_____

_____

Behaviors: _____

_____

_____

_____

Father: _____

Characteristics: _____

_____

_____

_____

Behaviors: _____

_____

_____

_____

Partner: _____

Characteristics: _____

_____

_____

_____

Behaviors: _____

_____

_____

_____

Prior to doing this exercise, you may have recognized the connection between one of your parents and your partner, or maybe your partner has some characteristics and behaviors of each of your parents. The purpose of this exercise is to bring as much awareness as possible to the connection between your childhood relationships and experiences, and your current relationship with your partner. This is one more step on the way to achieving the goal of having a healthier relationship.

Now it is time to take a relationship history. This will reveal patterns in your choice of partners.

Exercise 5.3: Relationship History

Fill out the following relationship history form. Include characteristics of the people that you were attracted to or in romantic relationships with, as well as significant interactions between the two of you and what caused the relationship to end. You may need to use separate sheets of paper to complete the relationship history.

Name: _____

Characteristics: _____

_____

_____

Significant interactions: _____

_____

_____

_____

Reason the relationship ended: _____

_____

_____

_____

Name: _____

Characteristics: _____

_____

Significant interactions: _____

_____

_____

_____

Reason the relationship ended: _____

_____

_____

_____

Name: _____

Characteristics: _____

_____

Significant interactions: _____

_____

_____

Reason the relationship ended: _____

_____

_____

_____

You are looking for patterns in partner selection and partner interaction. This process may even bring a new awareness to your current relationship and your interactions with your partner.

Schema Maintenance

Schemas are very resilient and very resistant to change. In fact, if they remain outside of our awareness, they are impossible to change. The first step toward changing a schema is to bring it to your conscious awareness. However, this alone is not enough to change your schema. Your schema is stubborn and powerful—so powerful that it has control of your thoughts, feelings, and behavior. Your thoughts are distorted by your schema, your negative emotions are escalated by your schema, and your self-defeating behavior is driven by your schema.

Remember the story about Brad and Lisa in chapter 1? Lisa lost her mother and father when she was young. Her relationship with her husband, Brad, was happy until he had to take a job in London. Brad's temporary move from New York to London triggered Lisa's abandonment schema. Lisa was flooded with negative emotions that fueled her cognitive distortions. While there was plenty of evidence that Brad had been nothing but a loving, attentive, and faithful husband, Lisa still concluded that Brad was having an affair with his assistant, Linda, that would result in his leaving Lisa forever, just as her mother and father had done when they had died.

On his side, Brad was confused and angry. Prior to this incident, he felt that he and Lisa had a strong, healthy, and loving relationship. They were both aware of her fears associated with her parents' deaths, but he did not expect her to treat him so badly when he had done nothing to deserve it. He was wounded and felt that their relationship had suffered a setback. For Lisa's part, she was playing right into the hands of her devious and powerful schema. If she continued to behave in an angry, possessive, and jealous manner toward Brad, he would leave her, thereby preserving her abandonment schema. The story of Brad and Lisa illustrates the power of a schema, even when both people in the relationship are aware of the schema and its origins.

The only way to reduce, de-escalate, or heal a schema is to replace the maladaptive and self-defeating behavior patterns with adaptive and healthy behavior patterns. In the next two chapters you will be asked to learn and engage in a number of alternative coping strategies designed to disarm your schema and your critical partner.

Summary

Schema coping behaviors are automatic behaviors that each of us develops as a way to avoid the pain that we experience when our schemas get triggered by another person or a situation. We use schema coping behaviors to escape the painful thoughts and feelings associated with a schema-triggering event. Unfortunately, these maladaptive coping behaviors only provide short-term relief from the pain of the schema, while also creating long-term negative outcomes for us and for our relationships with others.

Chapter 6

Alternative Coping
Strategies I

All relationships, even good ones, involve complaints and criticism. It's natural when they make a cameo appearance on occasion during an interaction with your partner. It's when they are in starring roles in the communication between you and your partner that it's harmful to the relationship. This chapter contains key coping strategies and techniques for minimizing complaints, ending criticism, and disarming your critical partner: deflecting criticism, calling process and not arguing content, the I-message, and listening—in particular, active listening and the awareness interview.

Keeping a Journal

During your process of implementing the alternative coping strategies that are presented in this chapter and the next one, I strongly encourage you to keep a journal in addition to filling out the forms and worksheets that are included in the book. It can be difficult to recognize progress in yourself, your partner, and your relationship when you feel so emotional. It is easy to get caught up in the moment and lose sight of the bigger picture and your goals. Your journal can serve as a reminder of where you have been and the steps that you have taken to disarm your critical partner. Some people are very good at keeping journals and can easily do this task, while others feel burdened by, or uncomfortable with, the idea of keeping a journal. If you struggle with journal keeping, there is a way to modify the entries that will ease the process for you.

Olivia is passionate about keeping a journal. She has been writing in a journal since she was twelve years old. It is second nature to her. Here is an except from her journal:

> David and I had date night tonight. I had hoped that we could have a pleasant evening, and I was prepared to avoid any topics that might be upsetting to him and result in another conflict-filled night for us. When I came downstairs, David said, "Why do you always wear your skirts so short? You look like you're going out with the intention of picking up guys at bars." My usual response would have been sarcastic and cutting: "Maybe I should be going out to pick up men at bars instead of going out with my husband, who doesn't appreciate me." But I paused and said, "Let me go change into another outfit."
>
> I hate the way that he criticizes my clothing choices because it really hurts my feelings, but when I objectively consider the core of his comment, I feel that he is telling me something that I need to pay attention to as I approach my fortieth birthday. I have been wearing the same short skirts since I was in my twenties. I probably need to adjust my wardrobe choices so that they are more age appropriate. I'm still not happy with the way that David speaks to me, but I really wanted to have a fun dinner out with him. His attitude toward me became more positive when I came downstairs in a nice pair of pants. I felt pleased with myself that I de-escalated a conflict between the two of us. Our dinner was more enjoyable than usual, although not without some of our typical tense interactions. Our night ended in bed with lovemaking for the first time in two weeks, so all in all, it was a great night!

That was easy for Olivia to write in her journal. If you are someone who finds this process challenging, here is Olivia's journal entry in more of a point-by-point format:

- *Date night with David tonight.*

- *Hurtful criticism about my clothing choice again—skirt too short.*

- *I did not react negatively back to him.*

- *Changed out of my skirt and into pants.*

- *Need to reevaluate my wardrobe as I near my fortieth birthday.*

- *Some tense moments at dinner but mostly positive.*

- *Ended with sex for the first time in* two weeks! *Great night!*

This alternative format requires less time and still highlights the key points of the interaction between Olivia and her husband. Both styles are easy to refer back to when you need the reassurance that you are making progress in your interactions with your partner.

Deflecting Criticism

Deflecting criticism is an important alternative coping strategy when dealing with a critical partner. Mindfulness is a key aspect of deflecting criticism. When you are in an active state of mindfulness, your attention is on the present moment. You are living in the moment, and you are observing your thoughts and feelings without making a judgment about their being either good or bad.

So how does this state of being look when you are dealing with your critical partner? You need to listen carefully to what your partner is saying to you. Listen to your partner's words and don't react too quickly. Take a deep breath. Try not to be defensive. Shut down your inner dialogue and avoid counterattacking your partner. Counterattacking will only escalate the unpleasant exchange. Dr. Aaron Beck (1999) explains that the counterattack is a natural reaction when we have been hurt; we want to hurt in return and restore a perceived balance of power in the relationship dynamic. Unfortunately, this retaliatory reaction will only succeed in escalating the conflict. If you are unable to respond to your partner calmly, the best strategy is to disengage. To avoid sounding defensive, it is important that you remain calm and avoid making lots of excuses, explaining, or accusing in response to your partner's criticism of you. Instead, take your time in responding to your partner. Process your feelings about what has been said to you, and if you feel that your response might contain a comment that you would regret later, then tell your partner that you heard what he said but need to think about it further before responding. If you feel that you can respond without counterattacking, then begin by acknowledging responsibility for any part of your partner's criticism of you that might be accurate. Follow this with an explanation of what you feel is inaccurate and unfair about your partner's criticism of you. As we saw earlier with Olivia, she was able to recognize that David had a valid point about the length of her skirts. His delivery was mean-spirited and hurtful, but his comment about her short skirts was accurate. Olivia was successful at staying in the moment and determining if there was any validity to what David had said.

If we read one of Olivia's older journal entries, we can see how her inner dialogue, defensiveness, and counterattacking escalated a conflict:

> Tonight we were heading to an engagement dinner party for Jim and Pam. I had just finished getting ready when David walked into our bedroom and said, "Is that what you're wearing tonight?" His comment immediately took me back to my childhood with my older sister, Ella, who has always been perfect and beautiful—and Mom's favorite.
>
> I tried so hard to get Mom's approval, but it never came. Her comments, even when they weren't critical, had a tone of disappointment. I was never good enough. I never looked as good as Ella. It hurt so much to be dismissed as "less than."
>
> I unleashed my anger on David: "So, I don't look pretty enough for you! I never do! I don't know why you married me! Oh yes, I do; it's because you aren't very attractive—you couldn't do any better than me."
>
> David looked stunned and shot back with "I am so tired of seeing you in those short skirts. I have been telling you for two years to stop wearing them. You're too old to pull it off without looking like a hooker."
>
> I ran into the bathroom and slammed the door. I felt so flooded with emotion that I couldn't think straight. After a few minutes I was jolted out of my emotional stupor by an angry pounding on the bathroom door. David yelled at me, "I don't want to be with you any more than you want to be with me right now, but we made a commitment to Jim and Pam, so we need to go." I looked in the mirror and wiped the tears from my eyes, and we left for the celebratory dinner.
>
> We rode in silence and avoided speaking directly to each other or making eye contact during the entire celebration for Jim and Pam. We were each the life of the party for everyone else, but we couldn't be civil to each other (if they only knew). We have perfected this painful routine. We rode home in silence. David grabbed his pillow and blanket in silence and made his bed on the sofa. I cried myself to sleep.

Clearly, the interaction between Olivia and David was painful for both of them. Much of the pain could have been avoided if Olivia had followed these steps for deflecting criticism:

1. Practice mindfulness.
   a. Stay in the present.
   b. Observe your thoughts and feelings.
   c. Avoid judgments of "good" and "bad."
2. Listen carefully to what your partner said.
   a. Shut down or ignore your inner dialogue.
   b. Don't react quickly.
   c. Take a deep breath and remain calm.
3. Don't sound defensive.
   a. Don't make excuses or explanations.
   b. Don't counterattack; don't say something that you will regret later.
4. Identify any accuracy in your partner's criticism.
5. Respond to your partner calmly.
   a. If you are able to respond without counterattacking or sounding defensive, start by taking responsibility for the part of your partner's statement that was accurate, and then discuss the part of the criticism that you feel was inaccurate and hurtful.
   b. If you cannot respond to your partner calmly, acknowledge that you heard what your partner said but need more time to think about it before responding.

Roadblock to Deflecting Criticism: Cognitive Distortions

Cognitive distortions play a significant role in perpetuating our schemas and triggering defensive and negative interactions between partners in a couple. When your schema is activated by a comment or a situation that reminds you of a past experience, the schema filter distorts the comment.

This distortion creates a misperception of a situation. The distortion confirms the schema and results in minimizing or denying any information that contradicts the schema. Behaviorally, the person reengages in a negative and self-defeating pattern with her partner.

One way to put an end to this cycle is to identify your past experience that gets triggered by your partner's comments or criticism. Try to be objective about your partner's criticism versus criticism you received from your parents. The following exercise will help you to identify the cognitive distortions that may be creating a roadblock to your ability to deflect your partner's criticism. A sample exercise that Olivia completed follows the blank exercise form.

Exercise 6.1: Identify Roadblocks to Deflecting Criticism

This exercise will help you identify some of the roadblocks that may be getting in the way of your ability to deflect criticism with your partner.

Identify the past experience that was triggered by your partner's criticism of you:

_____

_____

_____

_____

_____

Identify your cognitive distortion:

_____

_____

_____

_____

Identify your counterattacking comment:

_____

_____

_____

_____

_____

Identify your partner's constructive or accurate criticism:

_____

_____

_____

_____

_____

Identify the hurtful or inaccurate part of your partner's criticism:

_____

_____

_____

_____

_____

Now, let's look how Olivia completed that exercise based on her old journal entry.

Sample Exercise 6.1: Olivia's Roadblocks to Deflecting Criticism

Identify the past experience that was triggered by your partner's criticism of you:

When David commented on what I was wearing, it reminded me of how my mom always preferred my older sister, Ella, and how Mom always gave her compliments, loved the way she looked, and told her she was pretty. My mom never said that to me, no matter how hard I tried to make her notice me and compliment me. Other people would comment that I was attractive, but I never heard it from my mother.

Identify your cognitive distortion:

When David said, "Is that what you're wearing tonight?" I heard, "You look really unattractive. Why can't you look like Ella? She is so pretty." And I just felt like it was one more time that I had disappointed my mother.

Identify your counterattacking comment:

I told David that he married me because he isn't very attractive and couldn't do any better than me. I feel horrible for saying that to him, because I really don't believe it's true. I have always been so attracted to David, and lots of people have told us that we make such an attractive couple.

Identify your partner's constructive or accurate criticism:

David is right when he says that I shouldn't be wearing my skirts so short. I guess I am just having a difficult time accepting that I am not that young girl who could successfully pull off the look that was my trademark for so long. I am almost forty years old and need to accept that it's time to lower the hem of my skirts.

Identify the hurtful or inaccurate part of your partner's criticism:

When David said I was too old to wear my short skirts without looking like a hooker, it really hurt. I know I might be pushing the look beyond the appropriate age, but I know I don't look like a hooker. My clothes are very nice, and I take great care in putting together my outfits.

This exercise is helpful because you can identify the key elements of your partner's criticism that remind you of your past experience. This makes it easier to understand what is at work, both cognitively and emotionally, and opens the door to make room for necessary behavioral change.

Calling Process and Not Arguing Content

Often, when anger is present, the discussion between you and your partner can get off track. When this happens, it is useful to shift away from the subject (the content) that you are discussing and change the conversation to what is happening (the process) between you and your partner. This coping strategy involves self-disclosure about your emotional experience. It is necessary to present your comments about the process in a neutral way so that your partner will not feel that you are attacking him. The following story about Jack and Kathy is an example of calling process and not arguing content:

❤ Calling Process and Not Arguing Content: Jack and Kathy

When Jack got home from work, he was already angry. He had been mildly annoyed when he couldn't reach his wife, Kathy, on her cell phone before leaving the office. It had been another busy and stressful day at the law firm, filled with meetings and demanding clients. He'd had to skip lunch because his most important client had needed to talk to him. Jack was starving and had called Kathy to make sure that dinner would be ready when he got home. He was trying to avoid one of their typical arguments by warning her that he was not in the mood for her usual delayed dinner. He had tried calling her from the car during his drive home, but there still had been no answer. By the time he walked through the door, he was so angry that he couldn't contain it.

Kathy met Jack at the door. She appeared to be oblivious to his attempts to reach her by telephone. She greeted him with a chirpy, "Hi, how was your day?" and he let rip this response: "How was my day? Well, maybe you would have a clue if you had answered your fucking phone. What could have been so important that you couldn't take my calls? How is it that you always make it seem like you're busier than I am? Do you have a stressful job like I do? Did you forget to tell me that you were elected president of the United States? All I want from you is a hot meal when I get home from a long day at my job, which, by the way, pays for the house we live in and the food you should be cooking for me! What do you have to say for yourself?"

Kathy responded by saying, "I feel emotionally unsafe right now because you have such an angry look on your face and are yelling at me and hurting my feelings with the statements you're making. I'm sorry that you weren't able to reach me on my cell phone. I dropped my phone this morning, and it broke. I should have called you and told you. I'm sorry that you are so upset. Dinner will be ready in ten minutes."

Jack left the room and came back when Kathy told him that dinner was ready. He had clearly calmed down. Kathy had successfully de-escalated the conflict by calling process and not arguing content. Previously, in similar encounters with Jack, Kathy had responded by telling him that he was an angry, frustrated man who was unhappy with his path in life and blamed her for everything. Those retaliatory comments only escalated the conflict and provided no resolution.

When couples engage in name-calling, blaming, bullying, and devaluing, it is a guarantee that the fight will escalate.

The I-Message

Another successful strategy for de-escalating conflict between you and your partner is to limit your communications to "I" phrases to avoid being critical or attacking. John Gottman (1994) introduced the I-message as a nonblaming strategy for couples to express their feelings without falling into the trap of attacking each other. The I-message was created as a healthy communication tool for couples who are engaged in one or more of what Gottman termed "the four horsemen of the Apocalypse." His four horsemen represent four patterns of negative communication—criticism, contempt, defensiveness, and stonewalling—that lead to relationship breakdown. Using I-messages will prevent escalation of the conflict and retaliation by your partner. The use of I-messages is a way for you to express yourself without attacking your partner. With I-messages, you take responsibility for your own feelings and describe your experience without blaming your partner. This is a way to express what you want and need so that your partner can understand that her behavior is hurting you. And when your partner uses I-messages, it will help you understand what he wants and needs, thereby maximizing your opportunities to meet each other's needs without sacrificing your relationship. It is important that your I-message not contain a you-message.

♥ The I-Message: Jack and Kathy

When Kathy asked Jack to start using I-messages, it was not an easy transition for him. Jack had a temper and was quick to lash out at Kathy when things weren't going his way. Kathy was worn down from years of this treatment and longed for a more loving and kind connection between the two of them. She explained to Jack her feelings about the way he treated her when he was having a negative emotional reaction to people, situations, and events. She felt as if he blamed her for everything, and she wondered what it would be like for him to express his anger and frustration to her without using the word "you."

Here's an example of how it would have sounded if he had expressed himself with an I-message that day:

Kathy: Hi, how was your day?

Jack: I'm really frustrated and angry. My day didn't go as planned, and I couldn't reach you on your cell phone.

Kathy: I'm sorry about that. I should have called to let you know that my cell phone wasn't working.

Jack: Well, not being able to reach you certainly fueled my anger and frustration.

Kathy: Why was it so important for you to reach me?

Jack: Because I had to skip lunch to take an important meeting with a client, so I was really hungry and wanted to let you know that I needed to have dinner as soon as I got home.

Kathy: But I always have dinner for you when you get home.

Jack: You are always late at getting dinner ready for me.

Kathy: I'm starting to feel as if you are going into "attack" mode with me. Can you please keep phrasing your statements using "I"?

Jack: Okay. Sorry about that. I feel that I need you to be more attentive to me when I come home from work. And I suppose, for me, it means that I would really like for dinner to be ready when I walk in the door.

Kathy: It is nice to hear you put it in those words. Sometimes when you say things to me in a negative or angry tone, I don't really hear the content.

Jack: I guess I get so frustrated and angry from my workday that I don't really communicate well with you.

Kathy: And I'm not listening well all of the time.

Jack: I can't blame you. Making angry demands may work in my law practice, but it isn't the most effective way to get what I want from you.

Kathy: I want to feel that I am making you happy and that I'm not a disappointment to you.

Jack: You aren't a disappointment to me. I just want to feel as if you are excited to see me when I get home.

Kathy: If we can have more conversations like this, I will definitely be more excited to see you.

Jack: This conversation made me feel better.

Kathy: Me too.

Listening

For healthier communication, an important skill to develop with your partner is listening. Many things can get in the way of your ability to stay focused on what your partner is trying to communicate to you. How many of us have been at a meeting or seminar where everyone is asked to introduce themselves and say a little bit about what they do and why they are attending the event? Every person in the room, if we are being honest, is only partially engaged in the listening process; the rest of their attention is focused on rehearsing what they will say about themselves, judging what the other participants are saying, comparing themselves to the other people, or daydreaming. We've all done it. And the blocks to listening get worse when we are engaged in an emotionally charged intimate relationship.

♥ Listening: Carl and Brooke

Carl and Brooke regularly fight about money. They both work and make similar contributions to the household budget. They have been smart with their savings and, despite their young ages, have managed to purchase a home and two cars and take several nice vacations a year.

But Carl regularly gets upset with Brooke about her spending habits. When Carl is feeling stressed about work and money, he notices all of Brooke's expenditures. On Brooke's side, she feels that she works long, hard hours at the office and therefore deserves to spend some of her hard-earned money on something that brings her pleasure or distracts from her work-related stress.

When they talk about money and their financial picture, neither of them listens to the other. Carl knows that Brooke will argue that she works hard and deserves a reward, and Brooke knows that Carl will talk about their previously discussed goals of saving X amount of money a month and cutting back on unnecessary expenditures. It's the same argument every time, and it ends the same way—with neither of them feeling heard. They are both creating blocks to listening to each other.

Matthew McKay, Martha Davis, and Patrick Fanning (1995) identified twelve blocks to listening, all of which get in the way of truly understanding what is being communicated to us:

- *Comparing:* The listening gets distorted because the recipient is focused on how she or her experience or situation compares to the speaker or his situation.

- *Mind reading:* This block distorts the communication because the listener is focused on figuring out the speaker's "real" thoughts and feelings.

- *Rehearsing:* This block distorts the communication because the listener is busy rehearsing what she will say in response to the speaker.

- *Filtering:* This block distorts the communication because the listener may stop listening or let his mind wander when he hears a particular tone or subject that he finds unpleasant.

- *Judging:* When the listener quickly judges what is being communicated, she stops listening and misses the full content or meaning, thereby distorting the message.

- *Dreaming:* This block distorts the communication because the listener is daydreaming.

- *Identifying:* This block distorts the communication because the listener interrupts to share his experience. The speaker is never able to fully communicate her story.

- *Advising:* This block distorts the communication because the listener interrupts with advice before the speaker has fully finished communicating his entire experience.

- *Sparring:* This blocks the communication because the listener is quick to disagree or debate.

- *Being right:* This blocks the communication because the listener will go to great lengths to not be wrong and will block any criticism or complaints that are voiced.

- *Derailing:* This blocks communication because the listener derails the conversation by changing the subject.

- *Placating:* This blocks the communication because the listener is focused on sounding nice and supportive but is not really listening.

We all have listening blocks. It's a bad habit and a roadblock to establishing healthy communication with your partner. In the following exercise, write down the ways in which you block listening to your partner. Then take a look at what Carl and Brooke wrote down for their listening blocks.

Exercise 6.2: Your Roadblocks to Listening

My blocks to listening to my partner:

_____

_____

_____

_____

_____

Sample Exercise 6.2: Carl's Roadblocks to Listening to Brooke

My blocks to listening to my partner:

Comparing: *When Brooke talks about how hard she works, I stop listening and start thinking about how hard I work.*

Judging: *When I criticize Brooke about her purchases, I know she will rationalize them, so I stop listening to her because I have already prejudged her rationalizations as invalid.*

Rehearsing: *When Brooke and I are arguing and she is criticizing me for something I've done, I am already thinking about what I will say in response.*

Sample Exercise 6.2: Brooke's Roadblocks to Listening to Carl

My blocks to listening my partner:

Mind reading: *When Carl criticizes me for spending too much money, I stop listening and focus on what he is really thinking and feeling about me. Is he having doubts about having married me? Does he think I'm irresponsible?*

Rehearsing: *When Carl starts to criticize me about my purchases, I immediately start to think about what I am going to say to defend myself.*

Identifying: *When Carl tells me about how stressed he is, I immediately interrupt him to tell him about all of the stress that I am under at work.*

The habit of letting blocks get in the way of listening to your partner makes it impossible to communicate clearly and resolve conflict in a healthy way. By bringing your listening blocks to awareness, you are one step closer to actively listening to your partner.

Active Listening

Active listening is a necessary skill for developing a greater understanding of your partner and her experience. As mentioned previously, cognitive distortions can trigger defensive and negative interactions with your partner. Confirmatory bias and so-called old tapes are two of the ways in which our schemas can get in the way of listening to our partners.

Confirmatory bias (Meichenbaum 1977) is the tendency to only recognize what supports our schemas. When an event or interaction activates our negative schemas, there isn't any room for the positive facts that could disconfirm the schemas. It is easier for us to remember the familiar negative experience that proves our beliefs about ourselves or our partners. This tendency to only pay attention to what confirms our schemas gets in the way of truly understanding our partners' words and actions.

Another schema-activated reaction is called an *old tape* (McKay, Fanning, and Paleg 2006). In the previous chapter, you filled out the Cognitive Consistency form (Exercise 5.2) in an effort to recognize and bring awareness to any similar characteristics, behaviors, or both between your partner and your mother and father. "Old tapes" refers to when you react to your partner as if he were your parent. Another term for this is *parataxic distortion*, coined by Dr. Harry Stack Sullivan (1953). The more powerful the emotions that get activated, the more likely it is that you are responding to your parent, not your partner. By recognizing that you are having a schema-triggered emotional reaction to your partner, you can change your self-defeating behavioral response.

Here are five signs that you are responding to old tapes (McKay, Fanning, and Paleg 2006):

- You feel an instant rush of intense negative emotion in reaction to an interaction with your partner. You feel as if you need to protect yourself.

- It's an old and familiar feeling. The emphasis here is on how familiar it feels.

- It's a recurring feeling (this is particularly associated with anger).

- You feel that you are mind reading. When you make assumptions about your partner, the assumptions are most likely based on your childhood experience.

• You feel a fear of abuse or rejection when there is no basis for the fear.

Active listening (McKay, Davis, and Fanning 1995) is a three-step process designed to increase healthy communication between you and your partner. Now that you have identified your cognitive distortions, confirmatory biases, old tapes, and listening blocks, you are ready to begin to practice active listening. You will be an active participant when you listen to your partner's communication. The idea is to be engaged and let your partner know that you are paying attention by asking questions and giving feedback without judgment. The two of you will actively collaborate in the communication process.

STEP 1: PARAPHRASE

When you restate what your partner has said to you to make sure that you understand what she is saying, it makes it more difficult for cognitive distortions, listening blocks, confirmatory biases, and old tapes to derail your communication.

Let's look at this dialogue between Olivia and David to see how paraphrasing works for them:

David: Why do you always wear your skirts so short? You look like you're going out with the intention of picking up guys at bars.

Olivia: In other words, you are uncomfortable with my wearing short skirts because you think I'm going to pick up guys.

David: I'm not saying you'll go out and pick up guys. I'm saying that when you wear short skirts, it looks like that's what you're going to do.

Olivia: Okay, so you find my outfit inappropriate for our dinner date.

David: Yes, that's how I feel.

When Olivia paraphrases back to David what he is trying to communicate to her, he feels heard; it de-escalates what could otherwise become an angry exchange, makes for clean communication that eliminates any misunderstandings, helps the listener remember what is said to her, and makes it almost impossible for listening blocks to get in the way.

STEP 2: CLARIFY

Clarifying is an extension of paraphrasing that involves asking questions to get more details about what your partner is trying to communicate.

Let's look at the clarifying portion of Olivia and David's conversations:

Olivia: Okay, I won't wear this type of outfit on our dinner dates. Are you okay with my wearing short skirts on other occasions?

David: No, I'm really not. I think they were great when you were younger, but they just seem inappropriate now.

Olivia: So, you want me to get rid of my short skirts?

David: Yes. I think you're beautiful, and you would still look sexy in something more conservative.

By clarifying what David is trying to communicate, Olivia is able to fully understand how David feels about her outfits.

STEP 3: GIVE FEEDBACK

Now it's time for the listener to share her thoughts and feelings in a nonjudgmental way. This is a time to let your partner know how you feel about what he communicated to you and how he communicated it to you.

Let's look at Olivia's feedback to David:

Olivia: Well, that was a little tough for me to hear.

David: I'm sorry if I hurt your feelings.

Olivia: No, you were telling me something that I think I already knew but was having a difficult time accepting because I'm turning forty in a couple of months.

David: Babe, you look great. You just need to find a new style that suits you and still highlights how beautiful and sexy you are.

Olivia: It was difficult for me to hear your message at times because your comments about my outfits seemed so cruel. I know that some of it had to do with my confusing you with my mother, but part of it was your tone.

David: I'm sorry if I hurt your feelings. I definitely could have done a better job of delivering my message to you.

The dialogue between Olivia and David is an example of the power of active listening. By using active listening, Olivia and David are able to avoid miscommunication, show that they both care, and validate each other's feelings.

Awareness Interview

The awareness interview is a natural follow-up to active listening. You will need to use your active listening skills when you conduct the awareness interview with your partner.

When your partner responds to your question, repeat his answer to ensure accuracy and understanding. The idea behind the awareness interview is for both partners to develop a greater awareness of each other and each other's experience. Our schemas can get in the way of this because they generate rigid opinions and perceptions of ourselves and others. When you understand your partner's feelings and her experience in the relationship, it is easier to make changes toward healthier interaction.

Allow at least an hour for the awareness interview. Pick a time when neither of you is in a heightened emotional state. Use the following exercise as a guide for interviewing your partner.

Exercise 6.3: Awareness Interview

This exercise is adapted from the "Couple's Research Form," in *When Anger Hurts Your Relationship: 10 Simple Solutions for Couples Who Fight*, by Kim Paleg and Matthew McKay (2001). To conduct an awareness interview, go through each of these items with your partner

Describe what the issue or conflict is for you:

_____

_____

What do you need or want that you feel you are not getting?

_____

_____

What do you fear regarding the issue or conflict?

_____

_____

_____

_____

_____

_____

What are your beliefs about the issue or conflict, and about me and my feelings or motives?

_____

_____

What options do you think that you have around the conflict or issue?

_____

_____

_____

What are you thinking about during the conflict?

_____

_____

_____

Now let's look at Brooke and Carl's awareness interviews.

Sample Exercise 6.3: Brooke's Awareness Interview with Carl

Describe what the issue or conflict is for you:

The issue for me is our financial situation and my feeling that you don't care about it or worry about it as much as I do.

What do you need or want that you feel you are not getting?

I want to see that you care about what I am saying when I tell you that I am stressed-out about our financial situation. I want to know that you are really listening to me and that you understand my anxiety and worry.

What do you fear regarding the issue or conflict?

I fear that you are not taking me seriously and that it will jeopardize our financial security.

What are your beliefs about the issue or conflict, and about me and my feelings or motives?

I believe that you do not take what I say seriously, that you don't acknowledge how anxious and worried I get about our financial future.

What options do you think that you have around the conflict or issue?

I feel that my only option is to impose serious restrictions on your spending so that you will at last see how serious I am.

What are you thinking about during the conflict?

I am thinking about what I need to do to get you to listen to me and to take me seriously.

Sample Exercise 6.3: Carl's Awareness Interview with Brooke

Describe what the issue or conflict is for you:

The issue for me is that you can get so stressed-out about money that you won't allow me to spend the smallest amount on something that will make me feel better after I've had a stressful week at work.

What do you need or want that you feel you are not getting?

I need you to understand that I need to feel that I can spend a small amount of my hard-earned money to make myself feel better.

What do you fear regarding this issue or conflict?

I fear that you will always monitor my spending, even though I contribute to our household income as much as you do.

What are your beliefs about the issue or conflict, and about me and my feelings or motives?

I feel that you overreact to our financial situation and that when I respond calmly to your freaking out, it makes you angry, so you punish me by telling me that I can't spend money on nonessentials.

What options do you think that you have around the conflict or issue?

I feel as if I have no option, which is why I end up just getting pissed off and resentful toward you.

What are you thinking about during the conflict?

I am thinking about what I need to do to get you to understand that I need you to allow me *some flexibility with my spending.*

Remember earlier in the chapter, when we looked at Carl and Brooke's blocks to listening to each other? The awareness interview is a healthy way for them to build empathy and trust around an issue that has created significant conflict in their relationship. The interview provides a format that gives each partner the opportunity to find out about the other's experience and try to understand the other's needs, fears, assumptions, perceived choices, and frame of mind.

Summary

As you experiment with and eventually adopt the alternative coping strategies presented in this chapter, you will find yourself becoming more connected with your thoughts and feelings, and with those of your partner. Changing old coping behaviors that are deeply entrenched, automatic, and largely unconscious and replacing them with healthy coping behaviors will not be easy. Keeping a journal will assist you in tracking your progress as you navigate new ways of communicating with your partner. Additionally, it will serve as a reminder that you have made the conscious decision to change the negative dynamic between you and your partner, thereby eliminating the unnecessary pain that maladaptive coping behaviors bring.

Chapter 7

Alternative Coping Strategies II

This chapter presents the time-out technique for de-escalating conflict and the fair-fighting strategy to use when you and your partner are ready to reengage. Two essential strategies will be introduced—compromise and core empathy—to help end the negative behavioral cycle between you and your partner and create a healthier and happier relationship.

Time-Outs

Using a time-out is an effective coping strategy for ending a negative interaction before it escalates and causes more damage to the relationship. The four-step process for using a time-out follows (adapted from *When Anger Hurts Your Relationship*, by Kim Paleg and Matthew McKay, 2001).

Four Steps to a Time-Out

1. Make the T sign with your hands in the same way that referees signal a time-out in sports.

2. The person who calls the time-out should be the one who leaves the room or the house. When discussing the time-out coping strategy, agree on an appropriate amount of time for the two of you to separate. Some couples may require a shorter or longer cooling-off period than the suggested one-hour period. The success of this strategy is dependent on both partners being available at the end of the agreed-on separation time.

3. Your individual task during the time-out period is to cool off. This may require a different type of activity for each person. You may need to experiment to find what works best for you and what is possible during your designated time-out period (for example, if your designated time is one hour, going to a movie wouldn't make sense). The best activity to try first is a physical activity—a run, walk, swim, or bike ride or yard work, gardening, or yoga—anything that you have found to be a stress reliever for you. Avoid alcohol and drugs.

4. At the end of your designated time-out period, get together with your partner and check in with one another to see if you have both cooled off enough to have a reasonable discussion about the issue. If the two of you feel that you are still too emotionally charged to have a reasonable discussion, then agree on a new time to discuss the issue.

♥ Time-Outs: Jessica and Max

In the early stages of Jessica and Max's relationship, they had minor conflicts that were quickly resolved, so they didn't feel that they needed any alternative coping strategies for dealing with their conflicts. As time went on and their relationship progressed, the conflicts lasted longer, and unhealthy interactions between the two of them quickly escalated. They knew what buttons to push with each other, and their arguments would get out of control.

It would usually start with Max criticizing Jessica, who would typically respond in a defensive manner, and then they quickly fell into their routine of keeping score ("You did this," "Well, you did that"). Jessica would feel very hurt and unfairly attacked, and Max had a difficult time taking responsibility for his role in the conflict. This was emotionally overwhelming to Jessica. So she would call a time-out, which, for her, meant that she needed to leave their home for a night or sometimes longer. Max knew that Jessica was staying at her parents' home, and they would check in with text messages and phone calls to see if they had both cooled off enough to have a reasonable discussion about the issue that had caused the conflict.

For most couples it may not be possible or necessary to have such an extended time-out period to de-escalate the negative emotions. It is important to figure out what works for each of you. Try starting with an hour for your time-out period, and make adjustments from there.

Fair Fighting

When you and your partner come back together to discuss your differences, it is essential that your communication be fair and peaceful. There are three key attitudes (adapted from *Messages: The Communication Skills Book*, by Matthew McKay, Martha Davis, and Patrick Fanning, 1995) that contribute to fair fighting:

- *Conflict is inevitable.* You and your partner won't agree on everything. There is no avoiding conflict, and conflict is okay if it is handled in a healthy way.

- *Both people's needs are equally valid.* You and your partner may at times want different things, but it doesn't mean that the needs of either of you are more important than those of the other.

- *Both people can win.* Working together, you can find a way to get what each of you wants without taking advantage of or depriving the other.

The following fair-fighting rules are adapted from *Messages: The Communication Skills Book*, by Matthew McKay, Martha Davis, and Patrick Fanning, 1995.

Fair Fighting Rules

1. Set a time to discuss the issue.

2. State the problem by describing your partner's behavior without blaming or name-calling. Keep your communication clean.

3. Stick to one issue. It is too difficult to address more than one problem at a time.

4. Express your feelings, but be sure to use I-messages so that your partner does not become defensive.

5. Propose change. Be specific, direct, and clear with your request. Avoid broad terms and attitudes. Instead request a very specific behavior from your partner.

6. Describe benefits. Tell your partner what the benefits will be of his changed behavior.

7. Prevent escalation if you feel that the conversation is not productive, and then take a time-out (as previously discussed).

8. End your conversation with an agreement, compromise, or postponement.

Your conversation with your partner may end one of three ways: your partner agrees to your proposed change, your partner offers an alternative or a modification of your proposal and you compromise, or you reach an impasse and postpone the discussion for resolution at a future date and time.

Compromise

When you are trying to reach a compromise with your partner, use the active listening technique from the previous chapter. It is important that you each fully understand what the other is asking for. A solution that only meets the needs of one of you isn't good enough. It won't work, because one of you will have your needs ignored.

Exercise 7.1: Arriving at a Mutually Beneficial Compromise

Identify your needs:

_____

_____

_____

Identify your partner's needs:

_____

_____

_____

Identify what you agree on:

_____

_____

_____

Brainstorm about potential compromises where your respective needs are at odds:

_____

_____

_____

_____

❤ Compromise: Carl and Brooke

Remember Carl and Brooke, from chapter 6, who were experiencing conflict about money? In their latest argument about money, when Carl was feeling really stressed about their financial situation due to the fluctuations in his commission-based salary, he told Brooke that they couldn't afford to use the cleaning lady who came to their home every other week. It would cut their expenses by two hundred dollars a month, and that was important to Carl. For Brooke, it meant that in addition to working ten-hour days and commuting two hours five days a week, she would be spending the better part of one of her weekend days cleaning. Brooke completed the previous exercise while the two of them discussed their needs and potential solutions.

Sample Exercise 7.1: Carl and Brooke Arriving at a Mutually Beneficial Compromise

Identify your needs:

I need to be able to do enjoyable things on the weekend in order to balance out my stressful
workweek.

Identify your partner's needs:

Carl needs us to cut expenses so that he does not feel so much stress about our financial situation.

Identify what you agree on:

We agree that our weekends will not be as enjoyable if we have to spend them doing the deep cleaning that our cleaning lady normally does.

Brainstorm about potential compromises where your respective needs are at odds:

Have the cleaning lady come in once a month.

Identify another expense that could be eliminated instead of the cleaning lady.

Have Carl do all of the cleaning since it was his idea to get rid of the cleaning lady.

Have Brooke work overtime to pay for the cleaning lady.

Carl didn't like the idea of doing all of the cleaning himself, and Brooke didn't like the idea of working overtime to pay for the cleaning lady. Carl couldn't identify another expense that they could eliminate, so they compromised by having the cleaning lady come in only once a month.

By going through this exercise rather than staying deeply entrenched and rigid in their respective needs to get their own way, they were able to reach a compromise that allows them to spend more time off together while respecting Carl's concerns about their financial situation and Brooke's need for leisure time.

Writing everything out and reviewing your responses together will be a useful and, in most cases, successful exercise.

Core Empathy

The main purpose in using a time-out is to get to a place where each of you can be reasonable and feel more open to understanding the other's needs and core emotions. You need to put yourself in your partner's shoes. This exercise is often more successful when you imagine your partner as the wounded child that she was rather than the critical adult that she has become. What is the source of your partner's pain? What is triggering your partner's anger? What events turn him into your critical partner?

In chapter 1 we looked at the critical-partner profiles, and in chapter 2 you assessed your partner's schema with the childhood history form and the two worksheets specific to your partner's schema. The personal stories also reflected the childhood experience of a person with each of the schemas. No doubt, you were able to relate to some of the pain, or feel compassion and empathy for the people and their challenges.

Exercise 7.2: Applying Core Empathy with Your Partner

When you are not upset or angry with your partner, write down all of the things that you love and appreciate about her. Reflect on your partner's childhood struggles and the obstacles that he has overcome. Think about your partner's core emotion in the context of her experience and how her core emotion was adaptive given her experience.

What I love and appreciate about my partner:

_____

_____

_____

_____

_____

♥ Core Empathy: Alice and Neal

Remember Alice and Neal from chapter 1? Neal has an emotional deprivation schema, and when his schema gets triggered, he copes by being critical and demanding toward Alice. She is left feeling like a disappointment to Neal. In the heat of these moments when Neal is actively employing his maladaptive coping behaviors, Alice questions why she is with him.

The exercise for applying core empathy is a way for Alice to highlight the positive qualities that Neal possesses and appreciate what he brings to their relationship. Core empathy is not intended to excuse bad or hurtful behavior. It is meant to create a connection between you and your partner's inner emotional world. The following is Alice's response to the exercise.

Sample Exercise 7.2: How Alice Applied Core Empathy with Neal

What I love and appreciate about my partner:

Neal can be very attentive and sensitive to me and my needs.

Neal enjoys engaging in conversations with me.

Neal and I enjoy the same activities.

Neal has allowed himself to be open and vulnerable with me at times, even though it is difficult for him.

Neal treats people with kindness and compassion.

We all struggle, we all experience pain, and we are all aching to have the people closest to us validate our experience. All of the techniques and strategies in this book were designed to end the negative emotional cycle that gets in the way of you and your partners being able to understand each other. In order to understand your partner, you must inhabit your partner's world. You must imagine how you would feel if you had experienced what your partner experienced in her childhood years. Empathy is a prerequisite for validation. You must be able to connect to your partner's experience in order to validate it.

Accept your partner's experience and accept that your partner's behaviors are the result of schema-triggering events. With understanding, validation, and acceptance, there is room for change.

Summary

The time-out technique and the fair-fighting strategy provide effective ways to create healthy boundaries when you and your partner are in conflict. The compromise exercise is a tool that you and your partner can use when you are at odds over an issue. And core empathy provides a way for you and your partner to make a deeper connection by understanding, accepting, and validating each other's experiences.

Conclusion

Using Jeffrey Young's schema theory as a framework for better understanding yourself and your partner will lead to increased awareness about your individual behaviors and the dynamic between the two of you. Uncovering your and your partner's schemas is a process that can lead each of you to have a closer connection with your inner emotional experience.

The fight, flee, or freeze response in reaction to a perceived threat is a natural human evolutionary response. The same is true with the response to schema pain: overcompensate, avoid, or surrender. Although these coping behaviors provide immediate short-term relief from the pain that results when a schema gets triggered, they result in long-term negative consequences for you and your relationship with your partner. The maladaptive coping behaviors described in chapter 5 interfere with your ability to get your needs met in a relationship. By replacing your maladaptive coping behaviors with the alternative coping strategies presented in chapters 6 and 7, you will get closer to reaching your goal of having a more harmonious, healthy, and happy relationship with your partner.

When you are trapped in the pain of your own experience, it is difficult to remember that you are not the only one struggling and suffering. It's easy to lose sight of the fact that understanding your partner's experience and being compassionate toward yourself and the person who is causing you pain can get you closer to your goal. Cultivating core empathy is an important component to living a happier and more fulfilling life with your partner.

Finally, this journey will not be easy. You have taken the first important step to making positive changes in your life and your relationship by recognizing that you want to make the necessary changes to help free you from the negative dynamic that you find yourself locked in with your partner. Applaud yourself for all of your efforts, have patience with yourself when you feel that your progress is slow, and be kind to yourself when you revert to old, deeply entrenched behaviors.

Plato said, "Be kind, for everyone you meet is fighting a hard battle."

References

Beck, A. T. 1999. *Prisoners of Hate: The Cognitive Basis of Anger, Hostility, and Violence*. New York: HarperCollins Publishers.

Gottman, J. 1994. *Why Marriages Succeed or Fail: And How You Can Make Yours Last*. New York: Fireside.

McKay, M., M. Davis, and P. Fanning. 1995. *Messages: The Communication Skills Book*. 2nd ed. Oakland, CA: New Harbinger Publications.

McKay, M., P. Fanning, and K. Paleg. 2006. *Couple Skills: Making Your Relationship Work*. 2nd ed. Oakland, CA: New Harbinger Publications.

Meichenbaum, D. 1977. *Cognitive-Behavior Modification: An Integrative Approach*. New York: Plenum Press.

Paleg, K., and M. McKay. 2001. *When Anger Hurts Your Relationship: 10 Simple Solutions for Couples Who Fight*. Oakland, CA: New Harbinger Publications.

Sullivan, H. S. 1953. *The Interpersonal Theory of Psychiatry*. Reissued 1997. New York: W. W. Norton and Company.

Young, J. E. 2004. "Schema Therapy for Couples." Workshop, November 5 and 6, New York.

Michelle Skeen, PsyD, has studied schema therapy under Matthew McKay and Jeffrey Young. She completed her postdoctoral work at the University of California, San Francisco, and maintains a private practice in San Francisco, CA, where she lives and works. She is coauthor of the forthcoming *Acceptance and Commitment Therapy for Interpersonal Problems*.

Foreword writer Jeffrey Young, PhD, is founder of schema therapy, director of the Schema Therapy Institute of New York, and a faculty member at Columbia University College of Physicians and Surgeons. He is author of *Schema Therapy: A Practitioner's Guide* and *Reinventing Your Life*.

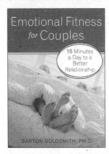
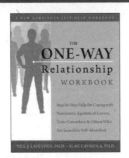